SUNDERLAND IN 100 DATES

ROBERT WOODHOUSE

The History Press

First published 2015

The History Press
The Mill, Brimscombe Port
Stroud, Gloucestershire, GL5 2QG
www.thehistorypress.co.uk

British Library Cataloguing in Publication Data.
A catalogue record for this book is available from the British Library.

ISBN 978 0 7524 7648 3

Typesetting and origination by The History Press
Printed in Great Britain

Contents

Acknowledgements

I am indebted to my wife, Sally, for her research and unstinting support and to Liz Taylorson for her administrative skills. My gratitude also goes to Bob Eastwood for information relating to railways in the Sunderland area and to the staff at Sunderland Library and Arts Centre and Sunderland Museum and Winter Gardens.

References for extracts appear at the end of each entry, and a full bibliography appears at the end of the book. All Internet sources are correct at the time of writing.

N.B. The Julian calendar was in use until Wednesday, 2 September 1752. The following day the Gregorian calendar was adopted, making the date Thursday, 14 September 1752. The dates in this book before and after the shift correspond to the respective calendars.

Introduction

The original settlement at Sunderland was established by Hugh le Puiset, Bishop of Durham who created a township covering about 220 acres on land close to the south bank of the River Wear. For several centuries it remained a small-scale fishing port until significant changes got underway during the late sixteenth century.

In 1589 Robert Bowes formed a partnership with a merchant of King's Lynn, Norfolk, to invest £4,000 in building ten salt pans with employment for 300 workers. The early decades of the sixteenth century also saw an increase in coal exports, which had reached about 80,000 tons a year by the outbreak of the Civil War in 1642. This rise in industrial activity had prompted a growth in the population of Sunderland to about 1,500.

During March 1644 the township was occupied by Scottish forces and Sunderland remained in parliamentary hands for the rest of the Civil War. The later decades of the seventeenth century brought continued growth in coal exports and in 1717 parliamentary legislation established the River Wear Commissioners, with powers to manage operations on the river from its mouth to Fatfield.

Towards the end of the eighteenth century an increasing amount of Sunderland's coal was transported in locally built ships and industrial growth spread across the river to the settlements of Monkwearmouth and Southwick. By 1801 Sunderland's population was in excess of 12,000 and improvement commissions were established in 1810 and 1826, with powers to levy rates for improving streets and sanitary arrangements.

With more than sixty shipyards by the mid-nineteenth century, Sunderland had become Britain's leading producer of wooden ships. Although the replacement of timber by iron (and then steel) vessels brought a reduction in the number of companies, more than 20,000 men were employed in Sunderland shipyards in 1900.

Other industries to prosper during the late nineteenth century included rope-making, pottery and glass-making, while the company founded by Cuthbert Vaux (1813–78) rapidly expanded to become the second-largest brewery in Britain. By 1901 the population of the Borough of Sunderland had reached 145,500 and its growing importance as an urban industrial centre had been acknowledged by the grant of county borough status in 1888, but the twentieth century soon brought a period of economic decline.

By the early 1930s, 29,000 male workers were unemployed, with a high percentage being shipyard workers. A number of factors, including foreign competition, hastened the decline of the shipbuilding industry and in 1988 the last Wear-based yard, North East Shipbuilding Ltd, ceased trading. Rope-making had already ended in 1968 and the closure of Wearmouth Colliery in 1993 saw coal exports cease, while the closure of Vaux brewery during 2002 marked the end of Sunderland's dependence on traditional industries.

The re-emergence of Sunderland was heralded by the granting of city status in 1992. Just a few years earlier, in 1985, Nissan had begun car production at Washington and a range of smaller companies became established on trading estates around the area, while a developing university complex gave increasing impetus to Wearside. This transition is perhaps reflected in construction of the National Glass Centre and (on the site of the Wearmouth Colliery) the Stadium of Light, home of Sunderland AFC.

Robert Woodhouse, 2015

SUNDERLAND
IN 100 DATES

12 January

St Benedict Biscop, originally known as Biscop Baducing, died at St Peter's, Wearmouth on this day.

Born into a noble family, he became an official at the court of Oswi, King of Northumbria, before leaving in AD 653 to pursue an interest in church matters at Rome. After a second visit to Rome he became a monk at Lérins in France, where he adopted the name of Benedict.

During a fourth journey to Rome in 671, he received instructions in monastic practices and three years later Benedict oversaw construction of the monastery of St Peter of Wearmouth.

Accompanied by St Ceolfrith, his successor at Wearmouth, Benedict visited Rome again in 678 and during 682 he supervised the foundation of St Paul's monastery at Jarrow. A further journey to Rome in 687 saw him add to an impressive collection of manuscripts, relics and pictures, which he endowed to his monasteries. The Venerable Bede was one of the scholars able to make use of the fine library that Benedict had assembled.

The feast day of St Benedict Biscop is held on 12 January.

(www.britannia.com/bios/saints/benedictbiscop.html)

3 July

An inquest on this day concluded that the death of stable boy Roger Skelton at Hylton Castle was 'accidental'. The castle's owner, Robert Hylton, was wielding a scythe during grass-cutting operations when Skelton was struck by the point of the tool. It is recorded in Durham Episcopal rolls, dated 6 September 1609, that Hylton was granted a free pardon.

Since those days, some four centuries ago, legends have arisen around the episode. Most versions suggest that Roger Skelton fell asleep in the warmth of the stables whilst preparing a horse for an important journey by Sir Robert. Annoyed by the delay, the knight is said to have smashed his sword into the stable lad's head, causing a fatal wound.

Before long, staff at Hylton Castle reported sightings of 'The Cauld Lad o'Hylton' and other strange incidents were attributed to his ghostly antics. Plates and dishes would be thrown around the kitchen or tools were found piled in a messy heap.

Acting on the advice of a local wise woman, staff at the castle were able to placate the ghost sufficiently to end the unnerving episodes, although reports of a ghostly presence persisted into the twentieth century.

(www.sunderlandecho.com/what-s-on/
was-the-cauld-lad-murdered-after-all-1-1141690)

4 March

On this day Scottish forces occupied Sunderland as the English Civil War reached a critical phase. Parliament and the Scots had signed the Solemn League and Covenant during September 1643 and the Army of the Covenant had gathered on the border during the closing months of that year.

Alexander Leslie, Earl of Leven, was in overall command, with David Leslie as Lieutenant-General of Horse and Alexander Hamilton in charge of the artillery train, while each regiment of the Covenanter army was accompanied by a Presbyterian minister. A strict code of discipline was also issued to the Scottish forces.

Although the size of the assembled Covenanter army totalled only about 14,000 men (which was much smaller than antici-pated), the Earl of Leven ordered them to cross the border into England on 19 January 1644. Their immediate objective was the City of Newcastle, which had considerable importance as a coal depot and as a supply base for weapons and supplies.

Adverse weather during the later part of January slowed the Scottish advance and the Marquis of Newcastle was able to march northwards with Royalist troops from York. It soon became clear that the City of Newcastle could now withstand a prolonged siege, so the earl led his forces southwards to complete the occupation of Sunderland.

(bcw-project.org/military/english-civil-war/northern-england/
the-north-1644)

22 June

An Act of Parliament on this day established a body to be known as 'The Commissioners of the River Wear and the Port and Haven of Sunderland' and granted it powers for twenty-one years. Members of the inaugural body included Anglican clergy, local gentry, coal owners, professional men and coal fitters (who liaised between coal owners and colliers).

Coal shipments formed a major proportion of increased trade from the port of Sunderland during the seventeenth century and, although attempts were made to improve the harbour area, the situation prompted coal merchants and coal owners to seek legislation for setting up an organisation to carry out essential work. Opposition from Tyne-based industrialists saw this move end in failure.

During 1716, Thomas Conyers and John Hedworth promoted a bill that was intended to develop Sunderland harbour and create a navigable channel of the River Wear, almost to Chester-le-Street. On this occasion opposition was overcome at the committee stage and again when the bill was considered by the House of Lords.

The first significant project carried out by the River Wear Commissioners was construction of a south pier, which began in 1723 and was completed in 1730.

(Glenn Lyndon Dodds, *A History of Sunderland*, 2nd edition, Albion Press, 2001)

5 September

On this day, Holy Trinity church was consecrated at a time when the port of Sunderland was growing rapidly. Design work by William Etty of York made extensive use of small bricks to give a sombre appearance to the exterior, but the interior was very light and spacious with seven pairs of large windows.

Sets of tall Corinthian-style columns supported the gallery and roof and the rector, Daniel Newcombe, funded the addition of the present apse in 1735. The west gallery was incorporated into the building in 1803 and it has three coats of arms on display. In the centre are the royal arms of George I, while on one side are those of Lord Crewe, Bishop of Durham and on the other the Bishop of London who consecrated the church.

During the early years Holy Trinity was at the heart of local government, with twenty-four gentlemen elected annually to regulate the parish's civil affairs under the chairmanship of the rector, but in more recent years congregations dwindled and the final service was held on 26 June 1988. Soon afterwards it was taken over by the Redundant Churches Commission and has been given Grade 1 listed building status.

(en.wikipedia.org/wiki/Holy_Trinity_Church,_Sunderland)

1 June

On this day the merchant vessel *Isabella* of Sunderland did battle with a French privateer off the coast of Holland. Under the command of Robert Hornby of Stokesley, she had a crew of only five men and three boys, and armaments that amounted to just four carriage guns and two light swivel guns, along with a few blunderbusses.

Isabella was at the head of a convoy that included three smaller vessels and about to enter port when a French privateer, Marquis de Brancas, appeared from among Dutch fishing boats. With a crew of seventy-five fighting men under Captain André and weaponry including ten carriage guns, eight swivels and 300 small arms, it had all the makings of a highly uneven contest.

After *Isabella* had run up her ensign the Marquis de Brancas ordered her to surrender with shots across her bow. The English merchantman replied with fire from swivel guns before her deck was raked with small arms fire.

Isabella's crew had already taken cover and the next hour saw Captain Hornby skilfully avoiding attempts to board his vessel. Eventually a group of twenty Frenchmen clambered aboard, only to retreat in the face of sustained fire from blunderbusses.

Isabella lost most of her rigging as fighting continued but it was the Marquis de Brancas that broke off the momentous naval engagement.

(North Magazine)

26 August

Nicholas Haddock, Keelman of Sunderland, was hanged at Durham for the murder of Thomas Alder, farmer, at Hilton Park House.

On the 21st of the preceding May, as Alder was walking in his fields, he was attacked by Haddock, who knocked him down, cut his throat from ear to ear and ripped up his belly. A young man, servant to Alder and coming that way with milk, witnessed the murder, whereupon Haddock threatened to kill him also. The lad immediately ran to Sunderland, and got assistance to apprehend the murderer. When he returned to the place where the deceased lay, the murderer was still standing by the body and swore he would kill the first person that came near him, at which the young man knocked him down with a stone, and the rest laid hold on him and secured him. Haddock, when in confinement, confessed to the crime and declared that he had no malice against Alder, nor ever saw him before in his life to his knowledge. At the place of execution, he said he was distracted at the time when he did the fatal deed.

(M.A. Richardson, *The Local Historian's Table Book* ..., M.A. Richardson [publisher], 1841–1846)

22 March

One of Sunderland's best-known heroes, Jack Crawford, was born on this day at Pottery Bank (then called Thornhill's Bank), in the eastern sector of the town. His father trained him as a keelman but in 1786 he was press-ganged into the Royal Navy and served on HMS *Venerable* under Admiral Duncan, Royal Navy Commander-in-Chief of the North Seas.

His finest moment came on 11 October 1797, when the colours of Admiral Duncan on his flagship were raked by Dutch gunfire during the Battle of Camperdown. Crawford climbed the mast of HMS *Venerable* and, in the midst of enemy gunfire, nailed the colours to the upper mast.

His hometown recognised Crawford's bravery by presenting him with a silver medal bearing the engraving 'The town of Sunderland for gallant services the 11th October 1797.' He also received an annual pension of £30 following an audience with King George III.

After his discharge from the navy, Jack Crawford returned to Sunderland, where he worked as a keelman. In spite of his pension, he was always in poverty and died during a cholera epidemic on 10 November 1831.

During 1890, a monument showing Jack Crawford nailing the flag to the mast was erected in Sunderland's Mowbray Park.

(www.sunderland-antiquarians.org/members-area/jack-crawford)

9 August

On this day the Wearmouth Bridge was officially opened by His Royal Highness Prince William, Duke of Gloucester in the presence of around 80,000 spectators. Until this time, development had been restricted by the lack of a bridge across the Wear in the locality (with the nearest at Chester-le-Street) and its design had to allow the passage of high-masted ships whilst spanning the 250ft-wide river channel. Organisation of the project was in the hands of Rowland Burdon MP, who consulted many prominent engineers, and early schemes favoured a stone bridge. However, when these became impractical, Burdon patented an iron bridge in conjunction with local engineer Thomas Wilson and financial manager Michael Scarth.

Work on bridge abutments began in October 1793 and the completed structure represented the world's longest single-span iron bridge. Total costs amounted to around £28,000 and tolls were charged for pedestrians (until 1846) and traffic (until 1885).

During 1805, stormy weather dislodged a number of the cross tubes and Robert Stephenson was in charge of major repairs between 1857 and 1859. By the 1920s the increased volume of traffic necessitated a replacement bridge, which was built around the old one, and opened on 31 October 1929.

(www.engineering-timelines.com)

25 May

William Paley, eminent philosopher and clergyman, died on this day at Bishopwearmouth rectory.

Born at Peterborough in July 1743, he was educated at Giggleswick School and Christ's College, Cambridge where he became fellow in 1766 and tutor of his college two years later. After ordination in 1767, William Paley achieved a succession of influential positions within the Anglican Church.

He opposed slavery and advocated prison reform, while his stance as a philosopher was utilitarian – with the belief that humans act morally to raise their overall level of happiness. During 1776, Paley married Jane Hewitt, with whom he fathered eight children.

His utilitarianism was explained in *The Principles of Moral and Political Philosophy*, published in 1785, and *A View of the Evidence of Christianity* followed in 1794, but Paley's best known work which appeared some three years before his death was *Natural Theology; or, Evidences of the Existence and Attributes of the Deity, Collected from the Appearances of Nature*. In this work he argued that God could be understood by studying the natural world.

Following his death, William Paley was buried in Carlisle Cathedral beside his wife.

(ncse.com/rncse/29/4/william-paley-1743-1805)

29 November

Sunderland was illuminated for three nights to commemorate the glorious news of Holland and Hanover being free from domination by France (during the Napoleonic era). On this night the town shone uncommonly brilliant when numerous devices and transparencies of 'Orange Boven', 'Wellington', etc. were displayed. The only drawback was the fury of the lower orders towards that very peaceable sect, the Friends, who would not light up, and numerous were the squares of glass that were broken each night: one Friend had every square of glass in his house broken, and at one time several empty tar barrels were in a blaze before his shop and house to the great terror of the inmates.

Members of the Society of Friends were based in Sunderland from the mid-1650s and most were involved in shipping businesses. It seems that they were soon in trouble with local magistrates for their activities, but in 1670 members bought land for a burial ground and constructed a meeting house at the site during 1689.

Although it was destroyed by a mob in the same year, it was immediately rebuilt and continued in use until 1825, when larger premises were opened in Upper Nile Street.

(John Sykes, *Local Records: or Historical Register of Remarkable Events* ...
Vol. 2, T. Fordyce, 1866)

20 March

On this day Galley Gill, near Wearmouth Bridge, was the setting for violence as angry keelmen vented their fury at the construction of coal staiths linked to John Nesham's Newbottle waggonway.

Earlier plans to extend the waggonway had been shelved because of opposition from keelmen but, following the completion of Nesham's line to Galley Gill, there was widespread talk of similar projects for waggonways and staiths. Colliery owners saved considerable amounts of money with such schemes but keelmen considered that their whole way of life at communities such as Fatfield and South Biddick was being put under threat.

The keelmen's destructive rampage began with the demolition of a bridge across the gill leading to riverside staiths. They then set fire to the timbers of the staiths and wooden hoists that lowered coal waggons to spouts for pouring coal on to ships. A nearby house was destroyed by the rampaging mob and roofs were ripped from other properties. During this episode, one man was fatally injured after being crushed by falling materials and the disturbance was only quelled by the arrival of soldiers from Newcastle. Damage caused during the violence was estimated at over £6,000.

(www.twmuseums.org.uk/engage/blog/the-newbottle-waggon-rail-way-map)

18 September

On this day:

Many of the tradesmen in Sunderland injudiciously refused taking the shillings and sixpences that were plain and without remains of the impression. In consequence of this, after dark, a large concourse of the poor inhabitants met and commenced an attack upon the shops of Messrs. Caleb Wilson, Nattrass, Middlebrook, Walton, Andrews, Hall and others all grocers and flour dealers; the windows of both shops and houses were nearly demolished, and the shop of Middlebrook completely gutted by the mob who were seen running away with hams, bacon and groceries. After the shop had been forced open, the brave 33rd regiment were called out, and on the riot act being read about midnight, they prepared to act hostilely, when the mob in a great degree dispersed but not before several soldiers received severe bruises from bricks. The house of Mr Barnes, surgeon, being at this time rebuilding, the mob took many hundred bricks for their destructive purposes; the town continued in great alarm and commotion for some time on this event.

(John Sykes, *Local Records: or Historical Register of Remarkable Events* ...
Vol. 2, T. Fordyce, 1866)

28 May

A diarist struck a harsh moral tone after recording a tragic incident on this day:

> A bull was baited at Sunderland, when a poor man, named Simon Thornton was thrown down by the crowd, and had his leg broken, of which he afterwards died. Several bull baitings had recently taken place at Sunderland. When will this cruel torture cease? Is there no punishment for wanton cruelty? If so, where are the magistrates? Such exhibitions are the disgrace of the vulgar, and are indications of a barbarous spirit which can only be eradicated by knowledge which rouses the finer feelings, and instils a sense of duty to every animated being.

Dogs used in bull baiting were specifically bred to torment and then attack animals such as bulls or bears. During the bull baiting it would creep as close as possible while lying close to the ground, before leaping in an attempt to bite the bull on its nose or head.

A bill to make this practice illegal was defeated by thirteen votes in 1802 but it was outlawed under the Cruelty to Animals Act of 1835.

(John Sykes, *Local Records: or Historical Register of Remarkable Events* …
Vol. 2, T. Fordyce, 1866)

7 October

A letter was published on this date in *The Enniskillen Chronicle &
Erne Packet* newspaper, in which Mr D. McDonald of Sunderland
claimed to have invented a 'self-moving machine' for travelling
on roads whilst carrying seven passengers.

He explained that it was operated by a system of 'treddles'
(treadles) with:

> ... a man sitting behind them working the same, and there is a fly
> wheel operating upon two cog wheels, which operate on a square axle.
> The man behind has little labour, as from the velocity of the fly wheel
> together with the aid of a lever which is in the hand of a person in
> front steering, he has not often to put his feet on the treddles.

The news report also indicated that after McDonald had improved
the 'friction of the body of the carriage' he would present his
machine to the Society of Arts with the hope that it would come
into common use (though he wished to make no financial gain).

Engineering journals of the early nineteenth century contained
numerous debates about the merits of the new range of veloci-
pedes but McDonald's must rate as one of the most extraordinary.

(archiver.rootsweb.ancestry.com/th/read/GENBRIT/2008-10/1223366508)

3 August

In consequence of existing differences between the ship owners and seamen of the port of Sunderland, the latter, on the above day, attempted forcibly to prevent ships going out to sea, when a most melancholy affair took place. A ship called *The Busy* was going out, with a number of special constables on board to protect the crew, when the men assembled in great numbers and attempted to prevent her by boarding. They soon overpowered the civil force, when a troop of the 3rd Light Dragoons from the barracks at Newcastle, who had been sent for some time before, to assist in preserving the peace on the River Wear, were called upon to assist the magistrates in getting the ship out to sea.

They succeeded in driving the intruders out of the ship, but in passing the north sand those on board were assailed with stones and other missiles from a numerous mob of men and women, which they bore with patience a considerable time; but one of the soldiers having been severely wounded in the face, they were ordered to fire in their own defence over the heads of rioters, but without the desired effect. Seven or eight shots were fired at the crowd by which three men were killed outright. Several were wounded.

(John Sykes, *Local Records: or Historical Register of Remarkable Events …*
Vol. 2, T. Fordyce, 1866)

15 June

Henry Watts, sailor and diver, was born on this day at premises on Silver Street, Sunderland. Like many contemporaries, he was drawn to a career at sea and at the age of 13 he sailed to Quebec as an apprentice on the brig *Lena*. It was during his stay in the Canadian port that another apprentice by the name of Nicholson fell overboard and Henry Watts made his first rescue.

During service on the *Cowan*, Watts saved the skipper's life after he had toppled out of a canoe and soon afterwards, whilst serving on the *United Kingdom*, he used a rope to swing out from the deck and rescue a boy who had been knocked over the side during heavy weather. Henry Watts' next vessel, the *Protector*, was moored in Woolwich harbour when two men were tipped from a nearby sand barge, and he was instrumental in saving them.

At the age of 36 and with a total of seventeen lives saved, Watts became a diver, and by his 42nd birthday he was credited with twenty-six successful rescues.

Seven years later, Henry Watt's total increased to thirty when he left his work on a dredger to haul a young boy from the Pemberton docks. By the time of his death on 23 April 1913, his selfless acts of bravery had resulted in eight medals and six certificates.

(North Magazine)

31 October

Joseph Wilson Swan, inventor of an early electric light bulb, was born on this day at Pallion Hall, Bishopwearmouth. From an early age he is said to have shown a keen interest in his surroundings and attended lectures at the Sunderland Atheneum.

At the age of 14 he was apprenticed to a pharmacy business and then joined a Tyneside chemical firm that produced collodion for use in the 'wet plate' photographic process. By 1871 he had developed a method of drying the wet plates that led to the age of convenience in photography. Some eight years after this he patented bromide paper, which is widely used in modern photographic prints.

Another of his research projects led to Swan's invention of a primitive electric light during 1860, but the absence of a good vacuum and an adequate electric source meant a limited operational life for the bulb and inefficient light. Following the improvement of vacuum techniques, Swan and Thomas Edison both produced a practical light bulb in 1880.

Further research led to Swan patenting a process for squeezing nitrocellulose through holes to form fibres and during 1885 he exhibited equipment for this process and items made from the artificial fibres. He was knighted in 1904 at Warlingham, Surrey and died on 27 May 1914.

(www.britannica.com/EBchecked/topic/576273/Sir-Joseph-Wilson-Swan)

28 April

Sunderland and its neighbourhood were visited by an awful storm of thunder and lightning, accompanied with a high wind. Part of the gable end of a house in the High Street, belonging to Mr Michael Reed, was blown down with a tremendous crash, on the roof of a public house, which it stove in and did considerable damage. The sloop *Bee*, of Blyth, laden with limestone, from Sunderland to Blyth, was obliged to put back for Sunderland, having lost the whole of her canvas at sea in a most tremendous gale of wind. On returning she struck upon the bar, drove amongst the frame-work, and soon after went to pieces. Great praise was due to Mr Martin Douglas, coal fitter, and others, for their exertions in saving the crew. The schooner *George and Henrys* of Sunderland, laden with lime, for Scotland, went to sea at the same time as the *Bee*, and was obliged to put back. She made for the harbour, when, there not being sufficient water for her, she struck upon the bar and sprung a leak; the water then getting to the lime, she took fire, and afterwards drove up into the harbour mouth, where she sank.

(John Sykes, *Local Records: or Historical Register of Remarkable Events …* Vol. 2, T. Fordyce, 1866)

23 October

On this day William Sproat, a keelman who lived near Sunderland quayside, became ill. He died three days later. This was the first case in this country of cholera morbus after the disease had spread throughout Europe.

Attempts had been made to prevent its arrival, including extending quarantine to ships from Russia and the Baltic ports, and the Central Board of Health met on a daily basis between June 1831 and May 1832, but to no avail. When the local board admitted that victims were suffering from cholera, ships from Sunderland were placed under quarantine and trade on the Wear suffered a significant decline.

By late December, when the outbreak seemed to be over, there had been 215 reported deaths in Sunderland, but a serious outbreak in Gateshead at the end of the year led to another 115 cases and 50 deaths.

During 1832 the cholera outbreak spread throughout Great Britain and resulted in 32,000 deaths. Although parliament passed the Cholera Morbus Prevention Act in February 1832, few significant measures had been taken to prevent its recurrence and during the late 1840s, unhygienic living conditions led to another outbreak that claimed 62,000 victims over a two-year period.

(www.parliament.uk/about/living-heritage/transformingsociety/towncountry/)

27 August

The members of the Sunderland Political Union, and other friends of reform, celebrated the passing of the reform bills with a public dinner in a large field near Waterloo Place. The tables were arranged under a spacious canopy covering and were well supplied with beef, ham, plum puddings, etc. The price of the ticket was fixed at 2*s* but in order that the poorer classes might be able to join in the celebration, a subscription was entered into by some gentlemen that allowed a number of tickets to be disposed of at 1*s* each.

There were two bands in attendance, for whose accommodation elevated platforms were erected at each end of the covering; a platform was also erected for the ladies, a number of whom appeared to view the proceedings with much satisfaction. Toasts and speeches occupied the meeting until about 7 p.m. but the pressure and uproarious conduct of a crowd broke in upon the meeting, beggared all description and rendered the scene truly ludicrous. As scarcely a word could now be heard from the speakers, the chairman, accompanied by Mr Attwood, and the members of the council, adjourned to Miss Jowsey's, the Bridge Inn, from the windows of which the chairman and Mr Attwood again addressed a great concourse of people.

(John Sykes, *Local Records: or Historical Register of Remarkable Events* …
Vol. 2, T. Fordyce, 1866)

13 December

This day marked the official establishment of the Sunderland Poor Law Union, with operations directed by an elected Board of Guardians numbering thirty-four and drawn from eleven constituent townships. According to the 1831 census, the population within the union numbered 42,664 and settlements ranged in size from Tunstall (population seventy-five) to central Sunderland (17,060).

Several workhouses were already in use and during the early years Sunderland Union made use of the existing Bishopwearmouth Harley Street workhouse. Purchased by the Board of Guardians at a cost of £2,100, it was altered and extended at a cost of £2,726 6s 9d before opening on 20 April 1838.

A new workhouse was constructed at a cost of £15,300 between 1853 and 1855 and with accommodation for 500 inmates. Designed by J.E. Oates, the building enclosed two courtyards with males based around one side and females in the other. The first inmates, a group of 306, were transferred from the old workhouse on 13 October 1855.

Between 1867 and 1872 the site was enlarged by the addition of hospital buildings, Union schools with places for 200 children and lunatic wards. Hospital departments were again extended during the Edwardian era and by 1930 the workhouse site had been renamed the Highfield Institute and Municipal Hospital.

(www.workhouses.org.uk/Sunderland/)

25 November

On this date James Hartley was granted a patent for Hartley's Patent Rolled Plate, manufactured using a new cast-glass process in which his company specialised for the next fifty years. The Wear Glass Works had been set up in the Deptford district of Sunderland some two years earlier and traded as James Hartley and Company. Initially Hartley was in partnership with his brother John but on 1 January 1840 he acquired his brother's share and became a sole trader.

During 1864, Hartley built Ashbrooke Hall in Bishopwearmouth as a family home and held a member of positions on local bodies. During service on Sunderland Borough Council, he was twice mayor and he was also a magistrate, a member of the School Board and the Royal Infirmary Board. In 1865 James Hartley was elected as one of the town's MPs and on 31 December 1869 he retired from the business.

After trading successfully for more than half a century, Hartley's began to decline. This was mainly because of the company's failure to adopt new plate-glass manufacturing methods installed by rivals, but James Hartley Junior continued the family's glass-making tradition before handing over to the Wood family in the early twentieth century.

(www.nationalarchives.gov.uk/a2a/records.aspx?cat=183-dshw&#0)

13 January

Samuel Storey, who was to play a major role in the growth of Sunderland in the late nineteenth century, was born on this day at Sherburn, near Durham. After attending St Andrew's Parish school in Newcastle he trained at the Diocesan Teacher Training College, Durham, before becoming a master at the new Church of England School in Birtley.

During his time at Birtley, Storey became involved in activities in Sunderland and late in 1864 he left teaching to pursue business interests. An interest in politics led to his election to Sunderland Town Council in 1869 and eventually he became the leader of the radical wing of the Liberal party in the town. He was elected mayor in 1876, 1877 and 1880.

One of Samuel Storey's strengths was his organisational ability and as an outlet for his party's political views, he founded the *Sunderland Daily Echo* during 1873. During the 1880s he was instrumental in establishing a short-lived chain of radical newspapers and in 1881 was elected unopposed as Liberal MP for Sunderland.

Storey remained in this post until he was defeated by the Conservative candidate in 1895, but in 1910 he was elected after standing as a Tariff Reform candidate. Some four years before his death in January 1925, Storey was presented with the Freedom of Sunderland.

('Samuel Storey of Sunderland ...' Thesis;
University of Edinburgh, P.J. Storey, 1978)

22 May

On this day John Grimshaw, a major figure in the industrial development of Wearside, died at his home in South Street, Sunderland. After starting his working life as a joiner and turner, he joined Rowland Webster and Ralph Hill in establishing Grimshaw, Webster & Co., rope makers, in 1793.

Shortly afterwards he opened what was probably the world's first factory for machine-made rope in a four-storey building with power from a 16hp Boulton & Watt engine. Between 1796 and 1802, Grimshaw was granted three patents relating to improvements in rope making and by the end of the eighteenth century his company was producing about 500 tons of cordage annually.

In 1805 Grimshaw carried out repairs to the cast-iron bridge that had been built across the Wear during 1796. By inserting iron diagonal braces he stabilised the arches that were in danger of collapse.

During 1822 he was granted another patent for manufacturing flat ropes and with a growing interest in railways, Grimshaw supported initial plans for the Stockton and Darlington Railway and then supplied haulage ropes on the track's inclined planes. Similar ropes were provided for the Canterbury and Whitstable Railway.

His business interests also extended into owning ships and following his death, John Grimshaw and Co. continued to supply ropes for marine use and other industries.

(www.grimshaworigin.org/JohnGwRopemaker.htm)

2 December

On this day Charles William Alcock, one of the founders and earliest officials of the Football Association, was born at the family home in Norfolk Street, Sunderland. His father had extensive business interests in the north east but a family move to the south saw Charles enrolled at Harrow School at the age of 13, where his interest in sport was fostered.

After leaving school, Charles joined his father and elder brother in the marine insurance business and continued his sporting interest by helping to form Forest FC, one of London's first football clubs. In 1863 this club joined others in forming the Football Association and Charles Alcock served as its secretary for twenty-five years.

During 1870 he organised and played in the first international match (England *v.* Scotland) and in the following year the rest of the FA supported Alcock's proposal for the FA Cup competition. Twelve clubs entered the inaugural tournament during the 1871/72 season and as captain of the triumphant Wanderers club, Alcock became the first player to lift the FA Cup.

Other sporting interests included a term as secretary of Surrey County Cricket Club, where he played a major part in organising the first Test Match between England and Australia. Charles Alcock died in 1907 and is buried in West Norwood Cemetery, South London.

(www.spartacus.schoolnet.co.uk/FalcockC.htm)

19 June

On this day a railway station was opened at Monkwearmouth to mark the new Sunderland terminus for the Brandling Junction Railway, which had opened in 1939 to link Wearside with South Shields and Gateshead.

It replaced a timber-built station in Roker Avenue which had drawn unfavourable comments such as: 'the usual accommodation provided for civilised people was wanting at this, as at almost every other Brandling Junction Station' and it was also said to be where people were liable to suffer 'frequent breaches of public decency'.

George Hudson, Chairman of the Midland Railway Company, wanted to celebrate his election as MP for Sunderland in an appropriate manner and commissioned Thomas Moore, a noted architect on Wearside, to design the station.

For some thirty years Monkwearmouth station was busy with a variety of passengers as well as consignments of cattle and sheep, but when the North Eastern Railway Company extended the line across the River Wear in 1879 its importance declined significantly.

After the Second World War, sections of the station became derelict and a decline in passenger traffic brought closure for pedestrians in 1967. Complete closure followed in 1970, but the building was reopened as a museum by His Royal Highness the Duke of Edinburgh in 1973.

(www.sunderland.gov.uk/CHttpHandler.ashx?id=6951)

20 June

This day saw the official opening ceremony for Sunderland Docks. A large marine procession led by the harbourmaster's barge, local lifeboats and the brass band of the 33rd Regiment sailed from Hetton Staiths into the recently completed Hudson (or South) Dock. Spectators numbering around 50,000 had gathered to witness the spectacle and entertainment was provided by military and colliery brass bands, fireworks and assorted pageantry.

The ceremonial opening was performed at 11 a.m. by George Hudson, railway magnate and MP for Sunderland in his role as chairman of the Sunderland Dock Company.

Hudson had established the company in 1845, at a time when there was an urgent need for improved dock facilities to deal with increasing coal shipments. The North Dock, constructed on the Monkwearmouth side of the river during 1837, was unable to cope with the greater volume.

At precisely midday the first cargo of coal was loaded on to the *Welcome*, one of four colliers at the rear of the marine procession. An outdoor banquet had been prepared, with seating for 1,000 guests to witness the ceremonial loading and tables were then set again with a beef dinner for 400 workmen of the company.

(www.engineering-timelines.com)

31 July

On this day the first Wear-built emigrant vessel left the port of Sunderland. The *Lizzie Webber* carried a total of eighty-two passengers for a fare of £20 each and children half price. After a voyage lasting almost twenty weeks, the ship arrived safely in Melbourne on 15 December.

During the nineteenth century, Sunderland saw a significant increase in shipbuilding. In March 1814 there were twenty-three shipyards with thirty-one ships under construction, and an increase during the following year saw thirty-one building about 600 ships.

By 1840 there were seventy-six shipyards and during 1850 Sunderland-based firms built five times more ships than in 1820. Completed vessels were almost twice as big and yards had increased annual production from two to five ships. *The Sunderland Herald* described the town as 'the greatest shipbuilding port in the world' and in the years 1846–54 Wearside yards produced almost one third of all ships constructed in the United Kingdom.

Between 1820 and 1867, Sunderland shipyards constructed sixty convict ships that transported more than 18,000 convicted criminals to penal settlements in New South Wales, Norfolk Island, Tasmania and the Swan River area in modern Australia.

(cityofadelaide.org.au/the-ship/the-builder.html)

28 August

On this day Charles Dickens performed at the Lyceum Theatre in Lambton Street, Sunderland. This was one of several visits by the writer to Wearside and though he expressed concerns about safety aspects of the recently opened theatre building, he was fulsome in his appreciation of the reception from the audience.

In a letter to his friend John Foster, Dickens wrote:

> Last night in a hall built like a theatre, with pit, boxes and gallery, we had about twelve hundred, I dare say more. They began with a round of applause when Cootes white waistcoat appeared in the orchestra, and wound up with three deafening cheers. I never saw such good fellows. Stanny [real name Clarkeson Stanfield, a close friend of Dickens and noted local artist who had prepared some of the scenery] is their fellow townsman and was born here, and they applauded his scene as if it were himself.

Dickens also lived for a while at Cleadon House, on Front Street in the village of Cleadon, which some people have suggested was the inspiration for Satis House, home of Miss Havisham in his novel *Great Expectations*.

(www.northeastlifemag.co.uk/out-about/places/
sunderland_has_become_a_literary_wonderland_1_1569407)

24 April

Sir William Mills, inventor of the Mills bomb, was born on this day at a property in Wear Street, Sunderland. He spent his early years on Wearside and completed an apprenticeship with George Clarke, Marine Engineers, before spending seven years at sea. In 1884 he was awarded a first-class certificate as a marine engineer and his engineering skills prompted him to invent a simple, reliable method for engaging and disengaging ships' lifeboats.

After returning to a land-based career, Mills opened this country's first aluminium foundry at Atlas Works, Monkwearmouth. Some of Britain's first aluminium golf clubs, Metallic Golfing Instrument Heads, were manufactured at these premises, while another of his companies in Birmingham made castings for the motor and aviation industries.

Early in 1915, Mills' Birmingham factory began to make hand grenades. William Mills had spent a considerable time improving earlier grenades so that his version included a four-second time fuse, enabling the thrower to take cover before it exploded. These bombs were widely used by Allied forces during the First World War and his wide-ranging contributions to the world of engineering and armaments led to a knighthood in 1922. He died at Weston-Super-Mare in 1932.

(en.wikipedia.org/wiki/William_Mills_(inventor))

21 May

Mowbray Park was opened on this day by John Candlish, MP for Sunderland. Following an outbreak of cholera in 1831, a health inspector had recommended the creation of an area of parkland and a government grant of £750 was provided towards the overall cost of £2,000 for purchasing a sector of land from the Mowbray family.

The original park was extended in 1866 with the addition of a lake and terrace and during 1879 the winter gardens, museum and art gallery were built along the Borough Road side.

During the Second World War the park suffered severe damage during air raids and various iron structures, including railings and the bandstand, were removed to manufacture weapons. Areas of the park were also adapted to grow vegetables for the 'Dig for Victory' campaign.

Following the war years, the park suffered from vandalism and neglect but in 1994 a grant of £4 million from the Heritage Lottery Fund enabled a programme of restoration to get underway. Mowbray Park reopened in 2000 with gates designed by Sunderland-born Wendy Ramshaw and a new water cascade, fountain and swan house around the lake, which had been returned to its original shape. The park was voted 'Best in Britain' in 2008.

(www.sunderland.gov.uk/CHttpHandler.ashx?id=6912)

17 October

This day saw the opening of Sunderland Orphan Asylum as part of the provision for mariners and their families. It was constructed in the East End by the Freemen and Stallingers who owned the Town Moor, and capital for the project was raised by selling access rights on the Town Moor to railway companies.

A competition was held to choose designs for the building and although the London-based firm of Childs and Lucas was successful, a local architect, Thomas Moore, supervised construction work. His reputation was already widely established on Wearside through projects such as Monkwearmouth station (opened 1848).

The completed orphanage reflected the popularity of the Italian Renaissance style and the prominent central tower replicated towers at Osborne House, Queen Victoria's residence on the Isle of Wight. Queen Victoria took a personal interest in the orphanage by donating £100 towards building costs and requesting to see the plans.

Gates and railings surrounding the orphanage demonstrate its maritime links with waves, harpoons and anchors. They also have boys in sailor suits, representing how those in its care were trained for a career at sea.

(www.sunderlandheritage.org.uk/buildings.php?id=95)

28 August

On this day, Mary Ann Cotton married George Ward of Monkwearmouth. This was Mary Ann's second marriage after her first husband, William Mowbray, died of an intestinal disorder in January 1865. His life was insured by the British and Prudential Insurance Company and she received a payout of £35, which was equivalent to about half a year's pay for a manual worker. Soon George Ward suffered a long illness characterised by intestinal problems and died in October 1866. The family doctor gave evidence that Ward had been very ill but also expressed surprise that his death was so sudden. Mary Ann again collected insurance money.

After joining the family of James Robinson as housekeeper in November 1866, Mary Ann became his wife in August of the following year. Earlier in 1867, Mary Ann's own mother and three children in the Robinson household had died after developing severe stomach pains. Robinson soon became suspicious of his wife's activities and forced her to leave.

A bigamous marriage to Frederick Cotton ended when he died of 'gastric fever' and rumours soon circulated about Mary Ann's involvement in the series of deaths. Following a trial, she was convicted of murdering her children and was hanged at Durham on 24 March 1873.

(murderpedia.org/female.C/c/cotton-mary-ann.htm)

9 December

Events on this day at a property on Union Street, Sunderland had a violent climax. John Dolan and Hugh John Ward were lodging with Dolan's girlfriend, Catherine Keehan, and spent the late hours of 8 December drinking in the town. After returning at 1.40 a.m., Dolan sent Keehan to find more beer and when she arrived home, Ward made a comment to her before retiring to his room. Dolan continued to drink his beer before suddenly leaping to his feet to attack Keehan. She screamed for help as he attempted to drag her into the bedroom and Ward ran to help with an attack on Dolan.

Keehan left the house to summon police officers. They quickly moved on as the commotion seemed to have died down but the two men were soon exchanging blows again. Gripped by fear, Catherine Keehan leapt from a window to locate the officers and when they returned, Ward had suffered a fatal stab wound.

John Dolan was taken into custody and tried at Durham Assizes during February 1869. Following a guilty verdict, Dolan was hanged on 22 March.

(www.genuki.org.uk/big/eng/DUR/D_Executions.html)

13 November

On this day a group of young men met at the Athenaeum and agreed to develop a local branch of the Young Men's Christian Association. (The national movement originated in London on 6 June 1844, with the stated aim of putting Christian principles into practice by developing 'healthy spirits, minds and bodies'.)

At a general meeting of the association in Sunderland during early December, a set of rules was adopted and an annual subscription fee of 5*s* was introduced. The opening meeting took place in premises on Borough Road Terrace on 15 February 1872, with the noted Arctic explorer Captain Joseph Wiggins acting as chairman. When he left Sunderland in 1874, his farewell gift was a boat so that the association could set up a sailing club.

Increasing membership brought a move to a larger building at the corner of John Street and Borough Road, where the opening ceremony in February 1879 was attended by MPs E.T. Gourley and Sir Henry Havelock, along with the proprietor of the *Sunderland Echo*, Samuel Storey.

Some fifty years later, Sunderland YMCA moved to a property in Park Terrace where Her Royal Highness Princess Marie Louise performed the opening ceremony on 5 December 1928. In the 1950s, premises on Toward Road became the association's headquarters.

(www.sunderlandecho.com/history-nostalgia/
wearside-echoes-fun-at-the-ymca-1-4052077)

22 December

On this date the first edition of the *Sunderland Echo and Shipping Gazette* was printed on a flatbed press at premises in Press Lane, Sunderland. Funding for the newspaper was provided by Samuel Storey and business associates, who provided donations of £500 each to accumulate an initial investment of £3,500. Five hundred copies of the four-page issue were sold at 12 p.m. and 4 p.m. at a cost of 4*d* each.

Further investment was needed during the early stages and in July 1876 *The Echo* moved to new premises at 14 Bridge Street, Sunderland. Samuel Storey had founded the newspaper to provide a mouthpiece for his Liberal views and initially it faced competition from existing local newspapers *The Sunderland Daily Post* and *The Sunderland Times*.

During 1880, Samuel Storey became chief proprietor of the *Sunderland Echo* and in 1891 rivalry with *The Sunderland Daily Post* saw him successfully suing his opponent for libel during the Silksworth Colliery strike.

The twentieth century saw *The Echo* survive difficulties posed by the First World War and the depression years of the 1930s, as well as the destructive aerial bombardment of the Second World War.

In 1976, printing operations were moved to Echo House on the Pennywell Industrial Estate but, following a takeover by Johnston Press in 1999, a move to Sheffield saw the final *Echo* printed in Sunderland on 3 November 2012.

(en.wikipedia.org/wiki/Sunderland_Echo)

30 October

This day saw the launch of the clipper ship *Torrens* from the Deptford Yard of James Laing at Sunderland. Flores Angel, daughter of the ship's first master and part owner, Captain Henry Robert Angel, performed the ceremony and the vessel displayed an impressive figurehead, modelled on Flores by the sculptor Joseph Melvin.

Torrens entered service as flagship of the Elder line, along with her sister ship *Marlborough*, built two years earlier. They represented two of the finest wooden East Indiamen vessels.

Captain Angel made fifteen voyages between Plymouth and Port Adelaide, averaging seventy-four days for the outward journey. He also claimed a record-breaking sixty-four days for the route and during one stage covered 336 miles in 24 hours.

Following his retirement during 1890, Angel was replaced by Captain W.H. Cope, who made six return voyages to Adelaide. On his first voyage *Torrens* was caught in a mid-Atlantic storm that caused major damage and resulted in a detour to Pernambuco, Brazil, for repairs. She finally reached Adelaide 179 days after departing from London.

Joseph Conrad, the noted novelist, joined the crew of *Torrens* as second mate on 2 November 1891 and served on the vessel until 1893.

(www.sunderlandecho.com/opinion/columnists/
the-clipper-ship-torrens-1-1147795)

25 September

On this day the former President of the United States, Ulysses Simpson Grant, visited Hartley's Wear Glassworks on Hylton Road, Sunderland. During his two-day stay on Wearside, Grant had a number of other official engagements including attendance at a firework display in Mowbray Park, a banquet at Victoria Hall, a visit to the South Dock and an appearance at the laying of the foundation stone of Sunderland Central Library and Museum (which opened in 1879). The town's first public or free library had opened in the Atheneum during 1858 and initially offered only reference facilities. A lending section was introduced to the library in 1866.

Ulysses Grant held office as the eighteenth President of the United States of America from 4 March 1869 to 3 March 1877 after achieving the rank of general in chief for Unionist forces during the American Civil War. During the civil war years he had led his army to victories in many important battles, but his presidency was racked by controversy.

He was criticised by contemporary observers for not taking a stronger stance during scandals but later gained much more respect and credibility for his support for the legal rights of black people to vote and hold public office.

(Alan Brett, *Sunderland People and Places*, Black Cat Publications, 1990)

14 October

The first rescue by the recently formed Sunderland Volunteer Life Brigade took place on this day when an iron-built barque, *The Loch Cree*, was stranded in the teeth of a gale while being towed into Sunderland Harbour.

Some seven months after their formation in March 1877, the volunteers were alerted just before 10 p.m. and training routines were soon employed as a line was fired to the stricken vessel in order to rescue crew members. However, at this stage *The Loch Cree*'s crew decided to remain on board their ship so brigade members stayed on watch in case further assistance was needed.

At about 3 a.m. the gale-force winds increased in severity and the crew signalled to the shore for further assistance. The Volunteer Life Brigade fired a rocket with a light line attached over *The Loch Cree* and stronger ropes were then pulled through the waves by crewmembers.

Having secured these ropes, breeches buoy equipment was brought into action to complete the safe rescue, one by one, of eighteen crew members and a pilot. This final phase of the rescue was completed within one hour.

(www.sunderlandvlb.com/rescues.php)

28 April

On this day the Sunderland Tramways Company began to operate horse-drawn trams in Sunderland under the provisions of the Sunderland Tramways Order of 1878. The initial route covered the short distance from the Royal Hotel in Monkwearmouth along Roker Avenue into Roker and this was extended some six weeks later by a loop that extended as far as Christ Church and another line that linked to the docks area. Initial rolling stock comprised three single-deck cars, which were supplemented by two double-deck cars when the extensions to the system were completed.

During 1880–81 Sunderland Corporation completed additional extensions to the tramway system, linking it to the Southwick area, and these were subsequently leased to the company. Trials were also held involving three steam trams but these were stopped after only seven months.

By 1894 the fleet had increased to thirty-three tramcars and consideration was given to extending the system. Sunderland Council formulated a new agreement but this was never signed and the eventual outcome was that Sunderland Corporation was granted authority, under the terms of the Sunderland Corporation Act 1899, to operate its own tramways.

After purchasing the company on 26 March 1900, Sunderland Corporation closed the existing horse-drawn routes and began to electrify the lines.

(www.petergould.co.uk/local_transport_history/fleetlists/sunderland1.htm)

4 August

On this day, the North Eastern Railway Company opened a line from Ryhope Grange Junction across the river to Monkwearmouth and buildings were completed on the current site. Existing stations at Hendon and Fawcett Street were also closed at this time.

The newly opened station, known as Sunderland Central, had retaining walls on its east and west sides to enclose a cutting with lines running in northerly and southerly directions. A single entrance, which incorporated street-level buildings, was located at the north end but a second entrance and linking buildings was added some five years later at the southern end. An arched-rib roof covered the platform area but, along with buildings at the northern end, it suffered severe damage during an air raid in 1943.

Complete rebuilding of the station took place during 1965 and modifications to local stopping services saw passenger trains concentrated on one island platform. A further major refurbishment of the 140-metre platform areas was announced in 2006 in which Nexus, operator of the Tyne and Wear Metro, co-operated with the Department of Transport on a £7 million scheme. In addition to structural alterations, the modernisation scheme included an animated display formed by LED units and coloured-glass wall panels.

(en.wikipedia.org/wiki/Sunderland_station)

13 November

On this day Sunderland AFC played their first game, which ended in a 1–0 defeat against Ferryhill Athletic at Blue House Field in Hendon. At that time the team was known as 'Sunderland and District Teachers' Association Football Club' and its foundation was mainly due to the initiative of James Allan, a teacher at Hendon Board School.

In the early years the team wore an all-blue kit and changed their home ground four times in seven years before making a base at Newcastle Road in 1886. During 1881, the club's name was changed to Sunderland Association Football Club and non-teachers were allowed to join.

Another milestone was reached in 1885 when the club took on professional status and some three years later this led to the departure of James Allan. The year 1888 also saw the appointment of Tom Watson as Sunderland's first manager.

During these early years, Sunderland's matches were in local competitions and the FA Cup as well as friendlies against Football League clubs (which included a victory over the League champions, Preston North End, on 28 April 1899).

A successful bid to join the Football League saw Sunderland win the title in their second season by a 5-point margin over Preston North End. During the next season, they retained the title with a bigger margin of 11 points.

(en.wikipedia.org/wiki/Sunderland_A.F.C)

1883

16 June

On this day, a tragic event at Sunderland's Victoria Hall left a total of 183 children fatally injured. 'The Fays of Tynemouth From the Tynemouth Aquarium' held a 'Grand Day Performance for Children', which included 'Conjuring Talking Waxworks, Living Marionettes and The Great Ghost Illusion'. Tickets for the show stated that every child in audience stood 'a chance of receiving a handsome Present, Books, Toys etc.' and 2,000 young people filled the auditorium with very few adults present.

When the moment was reached for distribution of prizes, children from the gallery raced in anticipation down the stairs. At the foot of the stairway a door had only been partially opened and within seconds children were crushed by those arriving from the upper floor.

Numbers of children were rescued by the swift action of adults and others were able to save themselves. One young disabled girl wedged her crutch against the wall and prevented herself from being crushed but many others were less fortunate.

The number of fatalities reached 183 and there were scenes of panic outside the hall as frantic relatives raced to the scene. Soon after the tragedy, a disaster fund was set up and a memorial was erected in front of Victoria Hall. In 1934 the monument was transferred to Bishopwearmouth Cemetery.

Victoria Hall was destroyed by a German parachute mine during 1941.

(Alan Brett, *Sunderland People and Places*, Black Cat Publications, 1990)

14 September

On this day, the foundation stone was laid for construction of Roker pier and lighthouse at the mouth of the River Wear. The scheme had been put forward by Henry Hay Wake, Chief Engineer of the River Wear Commissioners, at a time when coal shipments totalled around 15,000 tons each day.

Sunderland harbour had developed from a small natural inlet into one of the largest coal shipping ports in the United Kingdom and an earlier structure around the mouth of the Wear was in disrepair. Wake's plan was to construct curving piers that would partially enclose the river mouth and the existing harbour fabric to create 125 acres of protected water for shipping, with work on Roker pier, the north arm of the outer harbour, completed first.

Construction work posed a series of logistical problems, which Wake overcame by designing innovative techniques and equipment. The pier extended 2,000 feet into the North Sea and before huge bags of concrete were deposited on the seabed, sand was cleared away from the bedrock. The pier itself was formed with 45-ton blocks that were lowered into place by a huge crane.

The whole project, including the lighthouse, was officially opened on 23 September 1903.

(northernarchaeologicalassociates.co.uk/profile/44-RP.htm)

18 May

This day saw the opening of Sunderland's Park Road Methodist church, which became the base for members of the Methodist New Connexion who had previously worshipped at Zion Street Chapel.

Designs for the Gothic Revival style building were prepared by John Eltringham, who worked on schemes for thirteen nonconformist chapels in the Sunderland area between 1876 and 1905. Availability of a larger budget, along with an imposing setting overlooking Mowbray Park, enabled Eltringham to design a more imposing structure than most of his other local church buildings. In common with several of his other commissions, he set a central door below a four or five-light window and a spirelet soared skywards at the corner of the frontage, while a school was attached to the south-east corner.

Galleries spread around three sides of the interior supported on cast-iron piers with decorative quatrefoils, while furnishings are of high quality. These include pews displaying painted numbers and brass rails, which provide storage for umbrellas in front of an organ housed in a Gothic-style case.

This fine church building survived the destructive air raids of April 1941 and retains fine stained glass in the windows of the north aisle.

(www.sunderlandheritage.org.uk/buildings.php?id=82)

30 May

This day marked the opening of the sports ground at Ashbrooke 'for the physical training and development of the human frame and the promotion of healthful exercises'.

Initially the 6-acre site, which is located on the south side of the city centre, was a base for cricket and rugby teams but since then it has become home for a range of other additional sports associations including bowls, tennis, hockey and squash. The ground contains Sunderland's oldest sporting structure, an impressive Victorian clubhouse that was completed during 1899 at an initial cost of £600. Since then it has been extended and renovated but still retains much of its late Victorian atmosphere.

Ashbrooke has hosted many momentous sporting occasions, including visits by touring test teams such as Australia, India and the West Indies. It became known as 'The Lords of the North' and during the summer of 1926 a Durham *v.* Australia match drew a capacity crowd of 20,678.

In recent years a sector of land on the western edge of the ground has been sold for construction of apartments, and a squash court adapted as a fitness centre. Further income is generated by the staging of annual fireworks displays and music festivals.

(www.livingnorth.com/northeast/sport/lords-north)

6 October

George Alan Maling MB, BCh was born at Bishopwearmouth on this day. After attending Uppingham School he gained an honours degree at Exeter College, Oxford before qualifying for MB, BCh (Bachelor of Medicine, Bachelor of Surgery) in 1914 and the joint diploma MRCS, LRCP in 1915.

Maling took up a temporary commission at the rank of lieutenant with the Royal Army Medical Corps on 18 January 1915 and five months later joined the 12th Battalion, Rifle Brigade as their Medical Officer. During September 1915, as warfare spread across the Western Front, George Maling was awarded the Victoria Cross for his actions at the Battle of Loos. The citation stated:

> For most conspicuous bravery and devotion to duty during the heavy fighting near Fauquissart on 25 September 1915.

Lieutenant Maling worked incessantly with untiring energy from 6.25 a.m. on the 25th till 8 a.m. on the 26th, collecting and treating more than 300 men in the open, under heavy shellfire. At about 11 a.m. on the 25th he was flung down and temporarily stunned by the bursting of a large high-explosive shell, which wounded his only assistant and killed several of his patients. A second shell soon after covered him and his assistants with debris but his courage and zeal never failed him, and he continued his gallant work singlehanded.

(www.ramc-ww1.com/profile.php?profile_id=11778)

7 March

At the Sunderland Petty Sessions on this day, Superintendents Isaac Burrell and James Oliver were summoned on charges of assault preferred by Mr Samuel Storey MP. The proceedings arose out of a visit by Mr Storey to 'Candy Hall' in connection with the Silksworth evictions during the previous month. The case against Superintendent Burrell, which was taken first was dismissed, on which the prosecution withdrew the charge against Superintendent Oliver.

The dispute at the Silksworth Colliery culminated in a general strike of all the collieries belonging to Lord Londonderry in the country of Durham. The county magistrates at Sunderland renewed evictions warrants in 155 cases, execution to be stayed for 21 days.

The evictions were carried out after workers had been on strike for four months. They claimed unfair treatment because they were members of a union and although evictions remained peaceful, residents barricaded their doors and banged pots and pans. Eyewitness accounts recorded miners being carried out of houses in their armchairs and attempts to delay the evictions included sprinkling pepper on curtains and hiding bricks in furniture to make them too heavy to carry.

(*Monthly Chronicle of North-Country Lore And Legend*, Part LIV, August 1891,
W. Scott, 1891)

11 September

Normal Friday night routines among families in the Hendon area of Sunderland were interrupted on this day as reports of a ghostly presence spread through the close-knit community.

Pupils had earlier left the classrooms of St Patrick's RC School to head along nearby Sussex and Coronation Streets on their way home, but by 9 p.m. hordes of youngsters were retracing their steps as levels of excitement increased. Speculation soon circulated about the nature and identity of the spectres that had been spotted behind ground-floor classroom windows and the streets were soon crowded by pupils of all age groups.

While younger children remained silent as they strained eyes and ears for an explanation, teenagers forced their way to the front of the crowd. The sound of breaking glass brought police officers racing to the scene but it was some time before they were able to restore a semblance of calm and investigate the cause of the near riot.

After picking their way through broken glass and debris in the schoolyard, the officers soon explained the reality of the ghostly reports. Two white statues had been positioned on a windowsill and gaslights within a butcher's shop across the road had highlighted the statues in a shimmering glow.

(Sunderland Echo)

17 December

On this day George Balmer, one of the most famous names in the history of music hall and variety, was born in Sunderland. Better known as Wee Georgie Wood, he was only 4 feet 9 inches tall when fully grown and specialised in little-boy characters during a stage career that began when he was 5 years old and spanned more than fifty years.

Well read and outspoken, Wood's works – which include books *I Had To Be Wee* and *Royalty, Religion and Rats* and his columns in trade publications such as *The Stage* and *The Performer* – have been described as a fascinating blend of sharp insight, gossip and prickly comment. (In addition, he was fond of expounding his views at Lodge meetings of the Grand Order of Water Rats where he held the post of King Rat in 1936).

During his career, George Wood produced more than forty different sketches, starred in fifty pantomimes and appeared in several straight plays. In June 1946 he was awarded an OBE in the King's Birthday Honours List for services to the entertainment industry. He retired from performing in 1953 and died on 19 February 1979.

(Roy Hudd, *Roy Hudd's Cavalcade of Variety Acts*, Robson Books, 1997)

22 June

Sunderland was a blaze of colour on this day in celebration of Queen Victoria's Diamond Jubilee. Flags, banners and streamers were highlighted by bright sunshine and the town hall was covered in illuminations with the wording, '*Nil Desperandum*' (Never Despair), 'Loyal Sunderland' and 'God Save the Queen'.

Decorations spread along buildings in Fawcett Street and adjacent roadways with the colourful spectacle including the Liberal Club, Constitutional Club, Sunderland Museum and park bandstands.

Local residents displayed brightly coloured ribbons and rosettes in celebration of the occasion and thousands of people of all age groups flocked to Roker beach from early in the day. The incomplete pier was opened to the public and brass bands provided musical accompaniment from adjacent streets and parks.

Pensioners visited Monkwearmouth Hall for a Jubilee tea, and sailors from Assembly Garth and Trafalgar Square gathered for a reception and a gift of tobacco at the Seaman's Hall. Occupants of Union Workhouse were presented with Jubilee medals and similar mementos of the occasion were handed out to children at the Orphan Asylum.

As darkness fell, huge crowds gathered in Fawcett Street to witness the illuminations switch on and bonfires were lit at locations such as Tunstall Hill and Fulwell.

(www.sunderlandecho.com/history-nostalgia/wearside-echoes-how-sunderland-celebrated-queen-victoria-s-diamond-jubilee-1-4590465)

18 July

On this day fire swept through Havelock House, premises for George Henry Havelock's drapery store, at the junction of Fawcett Street and High Street West. The fierce blaze soon spread to cause destruction and damage to twelve business properties in High Street West, eleven in Fawcett Street, twenty-two shops, offices and a Wesleyan Chapel in John Street and three shops in Bridge Street.

Attempts to deal with the inferno soon exposed the limitations of fire-fighting arrangements in Sunderland and it was largely as a result of the firemen's commitment that damage was not more widespread.

The alarm was raised by a local lad who alerted Sub Inspector Sanderson at the police station. He soon determined that Havelock House could not be saved and defined boundaries for containing the fire while summoning extinguishing apparatus from other police stations.

It was several weeks before the fire was totally extinguished after an operation which involved seven fire barrows, eighteen water jets and 9,600 feet of hose, as well as the River Wear Commissioners' boat *Fire Queen* and fire crews from the London and North Eastern Railway Company.

In the aftermath of the blaze, Sunderland Watch Committee made immediate moves to drastically improve fire-extinguishing arrangements for the town.

(*Illustrated London News*, 30 July 1898)

18 January

On this day Councillor J.C. Kirtley JP, Chairman of the Watch Committee, laid the foundation stone of Sunderland's police station and magistrates' court at a site on Gilbridge Avenue. During the first decade of the twentieth century, Sunderland was at the height of its prosperity and a competition had been held to provide appropriate designs for the courts, police station and fire station within the irregular plot of ground bordered by Dun Cow Street and the High Street on the south side and Gilbridge Avenue to the north west.

The competition winners were locally based architects William and Thomas Ridely Milburn, who had worked separately for many years with William based in Sunderland while Thomas was employed by Liverpool Corporation. After forming a partnership in 1897, their reputation grew rapidly and a commission to design Sunderland Empire Theatre was followed by a series of theatre projects across the country.

Aspects of Baroque style were popular during the Edwardian era and this is reflected in Sunderland's police station and magistrates' court, along with sterner features in keeping with the building's function.

During the early months of 2014 plans were put forward to incorporate the building into a city-centre music, arts and cultural quarter.

(www.macq.org.uk/the-history/the-magistrates-court/)

1 July

This day saw the opening performance at Sunderland Empire Theatre with a show that featured a range of local entertainers as well as acts from this country and overseas. A capacity audience of 2,700 was present for both shows on this momentous occasion and when lights for the first house were switched on at 7.15 p.m., patrons broke into a round of applause.

The orchestra then struck up the national anthem and as the curtain rose a local entertainer, Lilian Lea, sang 'God Save The King'. The next act was W. Fullbrook and Co. in 'Astronomy', described as 'A really farcical sketch scintillating with fun' and this was followed by routines performed by the child comedienne Maudie Francis, comedy duo Thorpe and Coe, comedian Charlie Kay, American 'musical tramp' Will van Allen and the Cyclonic Sousloff dancers.

Top of the bill was Vesta Tilley with three of her famous male impersonations: Piccadilly Johnny in frock coat and top hat, scarlet-coated soldier Tommy Atkins and an Eton schoolboy. These routines drew rapturous applause and a further sketch saw her appear as the Seaside Sultan, an office boy 'on the swank' during his holidays.

An innovative feature, 'a biograph box' which projected a 'moving picture', was unveiled as the evening's proceedings drew to a close.

(www.arthurlloyd.co.uk/Sunderland.htm)

19 July

St Andrew's church in Roker, widely regarded as one of the finest English churches of the early twentieth century, was consecrated on this day. Plans for the church had been prepared by Edward Schroeder Prior, who had become increasingly involved with the ideas and practices of the Arts and Crafts Movement, and building work got underway during 1906.

The final cost of the building work and original furnishings and fittings reached £13,000 and much of this was provided by John Priestman, a local man who had risen from shipyard labourer to millionaire.

Constructed for the most part of grey magnesian limestone from the nearby Marsden quarries, St Andrew's external dimensions are dominated by an 80-feet-high tower set between two short transepts at the east end. A huge dedication stone on the corner of the Lady Chapel has an inscription cut by the hand of Eric Gill and the interior of the church contains many more examples of the work of this brilliant typographer and calligraphist.

All the woodwork and wood furnishings in the chancel were designed by Ernest Gimson and completed by Peter van der Waals but the most eye-catching item is the tapestry. Woven by William Morris and Co. at Merton Abbey, it is a replica of an original Burne-Jones painting that features the Adoration of the Magi.

(Norman Duncan, *Guide Book: St. Andrew's Church*, St Andrew's church, Roker, 2007)

22 February

On this day Lieutenant General Baden Powell, founder of the Boy Scout movement, inspected the first-ever Scout parade on Garrison Field at Sunderland. The group had been formed by Colonel Ernest Vaux, a member of the well-known local brewing family, and became known as 'Vaux Own – Sunderland No. 1'. During proceedings at the parade he presented each one of the newly recruited scouts with a small 'fleur de lys', the insignia badge that later became an instantly recognisable emblem for the many millions of Scouts who joined the worldwide movement.

Garrison Field was located beside the drill hall, which served as a base for members of the Durham Light Infantry and the Territorial Army. It extended in a northerly direction from the fire station towards the court buildings.

For many years the Garrison Field was an extremely popular location for a wide range of entertainments, including fairs and commemorative events with an array of stalls, roundabouts and side shows along with demonstrations by the local strongman, Samson Besford.

In recent times the ground has become a car park to serve neighbouring buildings.

(www.macq.org.uk/the-history/garrison-field/)

10 June

On this day the Queen Alexandra Bridge was opened by the Earl of Durham, who was acting on the queen's behalf. Work on the double-deck rail and road bridge had begun some four years earlier to designs prepared by Charles A. Harrison, and construction was completed by Sir William Arroll and Co. Ltd of Glasgow.

An estimated total of 350,000 bricks were used in the project, along with around 60,000 tons of red sandstone from Dumfries. The total cost of £450,000 was shared between the North East Railway Company and Sunderland Corporation.

The bridge facilitated the transporting of coal from pits in north-west Durham to Sunderland and also provided better communications in the area by linking roads on either bank of the River Wear. A single span across the river channel resulted from a clause in the North Eastern Railway Act of 1900, which stipulated that the river channel had to be crossed by a single span with a clearance of 85 feet at high tide.

During the early years the railway bridge carried about 6 million tons of coal for export but, after a decline in traffic, it was closed in 1921 and dismantled in 1985.

(www.sunderlandhistory.co.uk/.River-Wear-ID6/Bridges-IDS7/
Queen-Alexandra-Bridge-IDI23)

16 July

Nathaniel Tristram Jackley Hirsch – better known as Nat Jackley – was born into a theatrical family in Sunderland on this day. His stage career began in the 1920s as a double act with his sister Joy and he then joined 'The Eight Lancashire Lads' before teaming up as the 'straight man' to comedian Jack Clifford.

Nat Jackley soon embarked on a career as a headlining solo comedian. Tall and thin, with excellent dancing skills, an off-beat delivery of gags and bird-like neck movements, he was destined for stardom. He appeared in three Royal Variety Shows and topped the bill in summer shows at all notable seaside resorts as well as the London Palladium. In addition he appeared in fifty pantomimes, with the last one at Newcastle in 1980 on the same stage where his father had performed. Fellow performers such as Roy Hudd recall that he was an extremely unorthodox dame with memorable, though unusual, Girl Guide and military line-up sketches.

In later years Nat Jackley became a highly respected television character actor who is perhaps best remembered as the granddad in *Spoils of War*. He died on 17 September 1988 in Coventry.

(www.answers.com/topic/nat-jackley-1)

21 October

On this day the Scottish-born American industrialist Andrew Carnegie performed the opening ceremony at Monkwearmouth Branch Library in Church Street. Carnegie had accumulated vast wealth through his extensive railway and iron and steel companies before funding construction of colleges, libraries and hospitals as well as more than 2,000 libraries in different parts of the world.

His requirement was that local government organisations purchased books and maintained the building, and Sunderland pursued Carnegie's offer with plans to build two branch libraries. In the event, there was sufficient funding to build libraries at Villette Road, Hendon (opened 19 October 1908) and Kayll Road (opened 21 July 1909) at Monkwearmouth.

During his speech at the opening ceremony, Andrew Carnegie said:

> The library is the cradle of democracy and the men and women who read there will become more intelligent and think more of themselves and their rights and privileges, have more respect and therefore respect for others.

He also met Henry Watts, the hero of many rescues, and said, 'I have been introduced to a man who has, I think, the most ideal character of any man living on the face of the earth. You should never let the memory of this Sunderland man die.' Andrew Carnegie was invested with the Freedom of Sunderland.

(Alan Brett, *Sunderland People and Places*, Black Cat Publications, 1990)

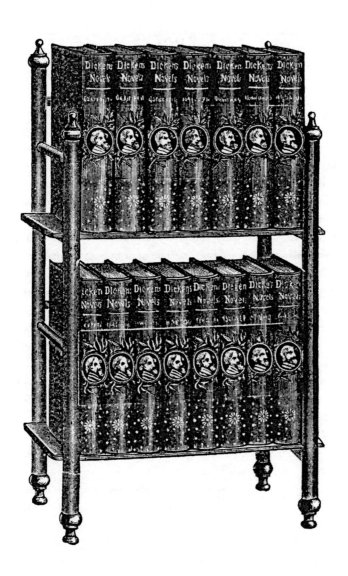

3 August

Sunderland East End Carnival began on this date as local residents decked their streets with flags for a series of events that lasted for a full week. Posters urged everyone to take part in the competition for the best-decorated house, with different categories and cash prizes offered for the best home decorated with plants and flowers, best illuminated house and men's and women's fancy dress competition. Judging took place at the Boys Industrial School, where other contests included breadmaking and weighing the heaviest baby. The most unusual competitions offered 'valuable cash prizes' for girls aged 16 years and under 'possessing the best and cleanest head of hair' and for boys and girls under 16 'possessing the best set of teeth'.

A tradition of holding festivities on the Town Moor was long established among residents of the East End with the emphasis focusing on blood sports such as badger, bull or hare baiting. There was also a brass band concert. In 1821 crowds assembled to witness a man walk on water – thanks to planks of wood attached to his feet.

During the nineteenth century, Silver Street was at the heart of annual celebrations on 21 June when local folk ate, drank and danced until the early hours.

(www.sunderlandecho.com/news/local/all-news/
carnival-capers-make-history-1-1076402)

21 January

On this day a German-built merchant vessel, the 1,624-ton *Orion*, ran aground at Roker Pier with a cargo of 3,000 tons of coal. The ship had just left the Wear and was heading for the post of Libau, on the Baltic coast, when its stern made contact with the White Shell Rocks and its plates and propellers were ripped away.

Crewmembers were rescued by personnel from the Sunderland Volunteer Life Brigade with assistance from the Royal National Lifeboat Institution (RNLI) lifeboat. The Volunteer Life Brigade was under the command of William Oliver, who was instrumental in setting up the organisation in 1877. Born in Sunderland in 1859, he volunteered as a lifeboat man at the age of 18 and acted as coxswain on scores of dangerous rescue missions. He became honorary secretary of the Sunderland branch of the RNLI in 1900 and among the many honours that he received, William Oliver was only the second person to become an honorary life governor of the RNLI in 1925.

Remains of the *Orion*'s superstructure broke into two main parts and were visible until about 1988, when all traces of the vessels were removed.

(www.searlecanada.org/sunderland/sunderland015.html)

1 April

The horrors of modern warfare were brought to Wearside on this day when German Imperial Navy Zeppelin L11 dropped high explosive and incendiary bombs on both sides of the river.

It left its base at Nordholz along with Zeppelin L14. Its original target was further south but the strength of the wind meant that L14 only crossed the coast to attack Tyneside at about 10 p.m. Following an earlier Zeppelin raid in June 1915, defensive positions around the River Tyne had been improved and difficulty in gaining height persuaded L14's commander, Viktor Schutze, to attack the more vulnerable port of Sunderland.

At about 11 p.m. the districts of Millfield and Deptford were bombed and after crossing the Wear the next target was Monkwearmouth. Bombs struck the goods yard and the roof over railway lines at the station was badly damaged. Further bombs fell on Thomas Street School, Victor Street and Whitburn Street, where St Benet's church was damaged.

A total of twenty-two people died during the night-time raid and several others died in the following days, while more than 100 local residents suffered less serious injuries.

The *Sunderland Echo* reported the raid on 'a north east town' by stating that three small fires had broken out but were quickly controlled while local people remained calm.

(www.twmuseums.org.uk/engage/blog/monkwearmouth-station-bombed/)

17 September

Novelist Mary Florence Elinor Stewart (*née* Rainbow) was born on this day in Sunderland. At the age of 5 she began writing and illustrating and after graduating from Durham University in 1938 with a First Class Honours BA in English, she gained a teaching certificate in the following year.

Between 1941 and 1945 she taught at Durham University and gained an MA in English. During 1945 Mary met and married Frederick Henry Stewart and continued with her part-time teaching until 1953, when she forwarded the manuscript of *Madam, Will You Talk?* to a publisher.

A contract with Hodder & Stoughton followed and the book was an instant success. Between 1955 and 1980 Mary Stewart published about one book a year, and each became a best-seller. She and her husband travelled widely and she included many of the overseas settings into her novels.

In literary circles Mary is widely regarded as originator of the modern romantic suspense novel, borne out of her ability to blend mystery with a love story. Many contemporary authors list her books among their favourites and acknowledge her influence on their own work but she has remained reluctant to categorise her novels: 'Can't I say that I just write stories? "Storyteller" is an old and honourable title, and I'd like to lay claim to it.'

(marystewartnovels.com/biography.html)

22 February

On this day Harold Richard Easby registered for military service at the Recruiting Office in Fawcett Street, Sunderland. He was aged 18 years and 4 months and during his school years he had displayed considerable academic and sporting ability.

After gaining a scholarship from the Bondgate Methodist Church Day School at the age of 11, Harold Easby took up a place at Darlington Grammar School, where he captained football and cricket teams as well as gaining awards that resulted in a place at Oxford University. However, instead of pursuing his academic career, Easby was selected for the Royal Naval Air Service, predecessor of the Royal Air Force, and was sent for training as an observer at Crystal Palace and then Redcar.

His first flight lasted 14 minutes on 17 May 1917 and less than a month later, on 10 June, he flew solo for 66 minutes at 2,000 feet. Five days later, a flight over Saltburn ended with a crash landing and in June 1917 he was moved to the Kent coast for training in photography, telegraphy and bomb dropping.

Success in his exams saw Harold Easby awarded two months' seniority in rank and he volunteered to serve on the front line at Dunkirk. Sadly he died on 7 January 1918 when his Airco DH4 tractor biplane crashed during a training exercise.

(*The Northern Echo*)

9 September

Sir Tom Cowie was born on this day in Sunderland, where his father and grandfather built, repaired and sold bicycles and motorbikes. During 1942 he joined the RAF and served in Coastal Command stations before a posting to India saw him based in the Sind desert outside Karachi.

After returning to Sunderland, he reopened a motorcycle shop during 1948 which featured a prosperous hire-purchase business. When demand for motorcycles declined in the early 1960s, Tom Cowie changed to Vauxhall car dealerships and the leasing and contract hire sectors soon became its main strengths.

During the late 1970s he became chairman and major share-holder of Sunderland AFC, but a serious slump in the club's fortunes resulted in relegation from the First Division in 1985 and Cowie cut his losses and sold out.

The acquisition of the Grey-Green coach line in 1980 heralded a period of growth for the Cowie Group but during the early 1990s, amid strained relations with fellow directors, Tom became titular president of the company.

He bought and developed a warehousing business in Sunderland but spent increasing amounts of time on grouse moors or overseas cruises. Tom Cowie was appointed OBE in 1982 and received a knighthood in 1992. He was a benefactor of his old school and of Sunderland University, where a campus was renamed in his honour.

(www.telegraph.co.uk/news/obituaries/9045286/Sir-Tom-Cowie.html)

13 July

On this day Sunderland's Chief Constable Frederick Crawley officially launched the first city-wide system of police boxes within his area. A local company, Binns, manufactured a box for each beat at a cost of £12 8s 6d and post office engineers installed wiring for the telephone. The interior of each box also contained a bench desk and chair or stool.

By the time the scheme was fully operational there were twenty-two boxes, and each of these compact structures, which resembled sentry boxes, had a direct telephone line to police headquarters.

During 1925 Frederick Crawley moved from Sunderland to take up the post of chief constable of Newcastle City police force. During his period of office he introduced the police box system to Tyneside and in the years that followed it was installed by police forces throughout England and Scotland.

Police telephone boxes and posts had first appeared in the United States of America towards the end of the nineteenth century, following the pioneering telecommunications work of Alexander Graham Bell. By the late 1880s, individual police boxes were being set up in Britain with telephones added to watch boxes within the metropolitan area.

(www.policeboxes.com/pboxhist.htm)

28 March

Black's Regal Theatre opened on this day on a site at Holmeside that was formerly occupied by the Olympia Exhibition Hall and Pleasuredrome. Built for the northern independent Black's circuit, this fine venue featured both live entertainment and films with seating for 2,500 customers. It was claimed to be the last word in comfort, with a lavish decor and luxury fittings facing a 57-feet-wide proscenium and 40-feet-deep stage backed by ten dressing rooms for performers. Other facilities included a cafe and roller rink and publicity claimed it was the first cinema 'to depend entirely on electricity for illumination'.

More than 5,000 people gathered for the opening night, where proceedings were led by the mayor, E.H. Brown. Entertainment featured Myron Pearl and Company along with the tenor Hugh Ormond, before a showing of *Out of the Blue* starring Jesse Matthews. Another element of shows at the Regal, which could extend to more than 4 hours, were recitals on the Compton organ by J. Arnold Eagle.

The popularity of shows at the Regal continued into the post-war years before decline set in during the 1950s and a takeover by the Rank Organisation saw it renamed Odeon in 1955.

(www.twsitelines.info/smr/13559)

8 December

Bruce Robertson, managing director of the book design and artwork partnership Diagram and founder of the Diagram Prize for the Oddest Book Title, was born in Sunderland on this day.

After attending local schools he took up an apprenticeship at a Wearside architectural practice, where his skills at drawing led to a scholarship at the Royal College of Art in London. Following his graduation, Robertson worked for several publishing houses before founding Diagram, with Bob Chapman, in 1960. Over the next fifty years the company provided graphics and other material for some 270 publishers around the world.

In 1978 he dreamed up the Diagram Prize to avoid boredom at the annual Frankfurt Book Fair and the first award was given to *Proceedings of the Second International Workshop on Nude Mice*. Subsequent winners have included *How to Avoid Huge Ships*; *Goblinproofing One's Chicken Coop*; and *Managing a Dental Practice: The Genghis Khan Way*.

The Diagram Prize is unique because judges do not actually have to read the books under consideration and since 2000 the winner has been chosen by a public vote on The Bookseller's website.

Bruce Robertson died on the day of presentation of the 36th Diagram Prize in March 2014.

(Daily Telegraph)

16 May

On this day Sunderland suffered 'one of the worst raids of the war' (according to the *Sunderland Echo*). Wearside shipyards were vitally important to this country's war effort through their crucial role in building new vessels and repairing damaged ones, and the local population lived under the constant threat of bombing.

The newspaper report continued: 'Showers of incendiary bombs as well as high explosives were dropped and these caused several fires, some of which burned furiously for a considerable time.' Several prominent buildings including the King's Theatre, the Dun Cow Street fire station and Avenue Paint Works were wrecked, while oil storage tanks at the South Docks Works of T.W. Greenwell & Co. suffered serious damage that put the dock out of use for several months.

By the end of the war, Wearside shipyards had constructed 25 per cent of the nation's total tonnage of ships, but the cost in terms of property and human life was considerable. It was reported that 267 people died in Sunderland during air raids and in the region of 4,000 homes were damaged or totally destroyed, leaving much of the town centre to be rebuilt in the post-war years.

(www.bbc.co.uk/legacies/work/england/wear/article_1.shtml)

19 September

Kate Adie, BBC news correspondent, was born in Sunderland on this day and was educated at the town's Church High School. Her studies continued at the University of Newcastle upon Tyne, where she gained a degree in Scandinavian studies before taking up a career with the BBC.

After a spell as a station assistant at BBC Radio Durham, she became a producer at Radio Bristol and then transferred to television where she directed outside broadcasts. Further work for regional news teams led to a post with the national news team in 1976 and she became a household name in 1980 when members of the Special Air Service stormed the Iranian Embassy. BBC coverage of the World Snooker Championships was interrupted as Kate Adie broadcast live reports from behind a car door.

During the 1980s she covered several other disasters and conflicts, including the American bombing of Tripoli in 1986 and the Lockerbie bombing two years later.

She was promoted to Chief News Correspondent in 1989 and held the post for fourteen years before becoming a freelance journalist.

Kate Adie was given the 'Freedom of the Town' (of Sunderland) in 1989 and received an OBE during 1993. She also holds honorary degrees from several universities.

(news.bbc.co.uk/onthisday/hi/correspondents/newsid_2625000/2625875.stm)

9 September

David 'Dave' Allan Stewart, musician, songwriter and record producer, was born in Sunderland on this day and attended Bede School in the town. His musical career began during his schooldays when he gained a record deal as a member of folk-rock band Longdancer, but success eluded him until the late 1970s.

During 1976 Dave was introduced to Annie Lennox and in the following year they linked up with another Sunderland musician named Peet Comber to form The Catch. Soon afterwards the band evolved into The Tourists and gained limited success during 1979 with a version of 'I Only Want To Be With You', before splitting up in the following year.

Stewart and Lennox continued to work together and formed the Eurythmics, who became one of the world's major pop acts of the 1980s. They were awarded the Ivor Novello Award for Songwriter of the Year in 1984 and Dave Stewart received Best British Producer award at the Brit Awards in 1986. The Eurythmics were introduced into the UK Music Hall of Fame for their outstanding contribution to British music and being an integral part of British music culture on 16 November 2005.

(www.allmusic.com/artist/david-a-stewart-mn0000629806)

9 September

This day saw the closure of the Hetton–Sunderland railway line, which had first opened in November 1822 in order to transport coal from mines in the Hetton area to staiths at Sunderland.

Measuring 8 miles in length, the Hetton Colliery Railway was the first complete line to be engineered by George Stephenson and the first in the world to be designed to use locomotives. Wagonloads of coal, eight at a time, and carrying over $2\frac{1}{2}$ tons each, were moved from Hetton to the Wear in about 2 hours.

Stephenson made skilful use of the terrain along the length of the line. Fixed steam engines were used for the steepest slopes, such as the initial sections from Hetton to Cope Hill and over the top of Warden Law Hill, while there were self-acting inclined planes for the few level stretches. Five of Stevenson's own locomotives were sold to the Hetton Company at the opening of the line but they did not prove to be reliable and were replaced by others during the 1830s.

The final set of wagons ran along the line on 9 September 1959 and removal of the track was completed some fourteen months later.

(durhamrecordsonline.com/library/hetton-colliery-railway/)

20 December

Fire swept through the Luxdon Laundry at Sunderland during the late hours, causing damage estimated at more than £50,000. The blaze was tackled by four units from the Sunderland area and reinforcements were summoned from six other brigades in County Durham and Tyneside including Hebburn, Seaham, Fencehouses and South Shields.

At one time, residents of nearby terraced properties were warned that they might have to be evacuated and one homeowner in nearby Ewesley Road described seeing 'an inferno' after she opened her kitchen door. Sunderland's fire chief, Leslie Allinson, reported that the fire was under control in about an hour and almost extinguished within 90 minutes.

The inferno was one of the biggest ever seen in the area but no one was hurt during the dramatic episode which left the laundry itself completely gutted. A spokesman for the company, Sid Parker, commented that all work would probably be stopped on the following day, although they might attempt to operate the dry-cleaning plant, which had been left undamaged along with boiler plants at either end of the premises and the administrative area. Directors of the company were due to meet on the site to determine future plans during the following morning.

(*The Northern Echo*)

4 March

On this day the official attendance at Roker Park for Sunderland's FA Cup sixth-round replay against Manchester United was 46,727, but it is estimated that the actual size of the crowd was almost double that total.

The gates had been closed early with the crowd numbering around 46,000 and, with many supporters fearing that they would not gain admission to watch the game, the ones at the Roker End of the ground were torn down.

Thousands of spectators poured into the stadium, with masses still outside the ground. Chaotic scenes resulted in a continuous line of cars for more than 12 miles between Sunderland and Newcastle, and Sunderland's players, who had spent the day at the Roker Hotel on the seafront, struggled to even reach the ground.

It is widely believed that this Manchester United game attracted the largest ever crowd at Roker Park but Sunderland FC's official highest attendance was recorded on 8 March 1933, when an incredible 75,118 spectators crammed into the ground for an FA Cup sixth-round replay with Derby County. Match day photographs show fans standing almost all the way up to the touchline.

(rokerreport.sbnation.com/2012/1/24/2723573/
trivia-tidbits-from-sunderlands-long-fa-cup-history)

1 July

At 3 p.m. on this day the final steam throttle was shut down at Ryhope Pumping Station. For three months short of 100 years, engines on the site had supplied water to the Sunderland area but the completion of impending reservoirs such as Derwent and Kielder, with lower running costs and production of 'soft' water, resulted in closure of Wearside's pumping stations.

The Sunderland and South Shields Water Company had been established in 1852 and as demand for water for domestic and industrial use continued to increase, 4 acres of land were acquired at Ryhope during 1864. Early in the following year Thomas Hawksley, engineer of the company, was instructed to prepare designs and specifications for the new works. Construction of the premises posed problems, as work on the engine and engine house had to be carried out together without interfering with the sinking of the wells.

Following closure in 1967, the engines remained unused for several years until the Ryhope Engines Trust was formally established in 1972 and the Ryhope Engines Museum opened as a static exhibit. During 1973 a trial steaming was held and at Easter of the following year the first public steaming took place. Forty years later, Ryhope Engines Trust marked the 40th anniversary of their first public steaming.

(www.ryhopeengines.org.uk)

1 January

On this day Sunderland Technical College officially became Sunderland Polytechnic. Following its opening at the Galen Building in Green Terrace during 1901, the college gained wide support from local industry and, significantly, it was the first establishment in England to introduce the 'sandwich course' that allowed engineering apprentices to gain higher qualifications whilst working. By 1908, twenty-five engineering companies were involved in the scheme.

During the inter-war period, funding from public bodies and private individuals facilitated considerable expansion of the Galen building and in 1939 the industrialist Sir John Priestman opened the Priestman Library, which had space for 10,000 books.

Special courses for the armed forces and Ministry of Labour personnel were arranged during the Second World War and with the development of new courses in the post-war era, an extensive building programme got underway. Completion of this work was marked by the opening of a new complex of buildings on Chester Road by His Royal Highness Prince Philip, Duke of Edinburgh, in 1964.

Creation of the polytechnic also included the School of Art and, later, Sunderland Teacher Training College, and another significant development took place in 1992 when Sunderland Polytechnic gained university status.

(www.sunderland.ac.uk/university/factsandfigures/ourhistory/)

5 November

During an official visit to Sunderland on this day, Her Royal Highness Princess Margaret officially opened Sunderland Civic Centre, which stands on 9 acres of land to the west of Mowbray Park.

The brown-brick building has two courtyards and a central tower set around two large hollow hexagons. It was completed at a cost of £3.5 million to designs prepared by the eminent architect Sir Basil Urwin Spence. The main entrance was located at the hub of the two hexagons and easy public access was provided by a railway bridge from the town centre or, on the east side, via a footbridge from Mowbray Park. Buildings were set on an upward slope from the northern end of the site, where no block was more than four storeys in height.

According to local press reports there were two embarrassing incidents during the official ceremony. The Sunderland Youth International Concert Band were unable to play a planned tune because five of the band's trumpeters were missing and when the town clerk came to present a set of goblets to Princess Margaret, they were nowhere to be found.

(canmore.rcahms.gov.uk/en/site/284670/details/
tyne+and+wear+sunderland+sunderland+civic+centre/)

7 May

On this day rock legends The Who appeared at the Top Rank Suite, Sunderland in a concert arranged by Fillmore North Promotions. Advertisements for the event outlined attractions including 'LATE BARS 8–1 A.M.' 'LATE TRANSPORT' and 'NO DRESS RESTRICTIONS' with tickets priced at '50p! YES … ONLY 50p.'

The Who enjoyed a series of Top 10 hits from the mid 1960s including 'I Can't Explain', 'Anyway, Anyhow, Anywhere', 'My Generation', 'Substitute', 'I'm a Boy', 'Happy Jack' and 'Pinball Wizard' and during the summer of 1971, soon after their visit to Sunderland, they returned to the charts with 'Won't Get Fooled Again'. Members of the group at the time of their visit to Sunderland were Roger Daltrey, lead vocals and harmonica; Pete Townshend, lead guitar and vocals; John Entwhistle, bass guitar and vocals; and drummer, Keith Moon.

This tour during summer 1971 saw The Who perform Pete Townshend's rock opera *Lifehouse*, much of which featured on their album *Who's Next*. It was also the first year that the group performed with backing tapes, which enabled them to include the synthesizer tracks from both 'Won't Get Fooled Again' and 'Baba O'Riley' on stage.

(*Sunderland Echo*)

5 May

On this day Sunderland recorded a dramatic victory over Leeds United in the FA Cup Final at Wembley Stadium. Leeds, the overwhelming favourites, were the cup holders and this occasion marked their third appearance in the final during the previous four years while Sunderland, FA Cup winners in 1937, were a second division team.

During the early stages of the match Leeds were held in check by the decisive tackling and interception of Horswill and Porterfield, but as the first half progressed they became better organised by the accurate passing of Giles.

Sunderland's defence, superbly marshalled by Watson, held the Leeds forwards in check while Madeley and Hunter were equally imperious for the Yorkshire side until the deadlock was broken after half an hour.

Harvey, the Leeds goalkeeper, tipped a long shot from Kerr over the bar and from the resulting corner, the ball reached Porterfield. He controlled the ball on his left thigh and then struck a right foot shot into the net.

The scoreline was to remain unchanged but this was due, 'in large part, to an incredible double save by Montgomery. He first palmed out a header from Cherry and then twisted and changed direction to tip the ball on to the underside of the bar. Sunderland resisted further Leeds pressure to achieve this highly memorable victory.

(www.thefa.com/competitions/facompetitions/thefacup/history/
historyofthefacup/1973sunderlandleeds)

26 December

This day saw the first Boxing Day Dip take place at Seaburn beach, with forty hardy individuals braving the North Sea's icy breakers to raise funds for local charities. The inaugural event was organised by the Sunderland Lions Club and since then, under their guidance, it has become an annual event with an estimated 1,000 participants supported by as many as 5,000 spectators.

Part of the fun for 'dippers' is dressing up, and teams are often made up from employees of local companies who arrive in themed fancy-dress costumes. After promenading along the seafront from the Seaburn Centre, with a competition to choose the best-dressed dipper, there is the headlong dash into the chilly waters. (Temperatures usually range from 4–10°C.)

The Mayor of Sunderland usually joins crowds of spectators ranged along the promenade and beach at Seaburn, and on Boxing Day 2013 dippers included Hogwarts pupils, video game characters, superheroes and penguins. An estimated total of £73,111 had been pledged in support of the great range of local charities, with the Lions taking a small share to fund their own good causes. (*Sunderland Echo*)

26 April

On this day one of this country's best-known comedy actors, Sid James, collapsed on stage at the Sunderland Empire with a heart attack and died soon afterwards. He was appearing in *The Mating Season*, a farce by the Irish playwright, Sam Gee, and his co-star was a life-long friend, Olga Lowe.

When James collapsed she thought he was playing a practical joke after he failed to reply to her dialogue, but when there was still no response to her ad-libs she moved towards the wings in search of assistance. The technical manager called for the curtains to be closed and summoned a doctor, while the audience responded with laughter in the belief that it was part of the show.

Sid James was taken to hospital by ambulance but died about an hour later, aged 62. Following cremation, his ashes were scattered at Golders Green Crematorium.

Born to Jewish parents in South Africa in May 1913, Solomon Joel Cohen (as he was born) became a lieutenant in the South African army during the Second World War and after the end of hostilities in 1945 he moved to Britain. His first appearances were in repertory but Sid James soon became a household name in the British film industry and was probably best known for the Carry On films. His ghost is said to haunt the Sunderland Empire.

(www.express.co.uk/news/uk/396943/
Sid-James-the-crimper-who-became-Carry-On-s-king)

8 July

On this day the first car to be manufactured by Nissan's Sunderland production line rolled out of the factory. The Bluebird saloon, which was donated to Sunderland Museum, had taken more than a month to assemble and it was hailed as a beacon for the north east's future economy. By the end of the first year, 430 production-line staff had assembled more than 20,000 Bluebirds.

During 1983 Nissan had become the first Japanese carmaker to build a new plant in Europe and through the first phase of its development in the UK, the company created 450 jobs and invested £50 million. By the end of the first decade of operations the workforce had increased to more than 1,600 people, with investment amounting to £560 million. At this point work began on the Primera.

In December 1998, a Nissan Micra – the 2 millionth car produced at the factory – rolled off the production line and by the early days of 2013 a total of 6,100 people were employed at Nissan works. During the previous year it had become the first UK car factory to manufacture more than 500,000 vehicles in a year.

On 28 March 2013 the prime minister, David Cameron, attended the official ceremony for the production of the ground-breaking Nissan Leaf electric car.

(*The Northern Echo*)

12 December

On this day the final ship to be built on the River Wear slid down the slipway at the Pallion yard. It marked the end of an industry that dated back to 1346 (when documents indicate that Thomas Menville was building boats on the river).

During the first two decades of the nineteenth century, the number of shipyards on the Wear increased from nine to fifteen. By the 1860s there was a total of fifty-eight yards building wooden ships and it is claimed that Sunderland shipyards provided more than a quarter of the nation's total tonnage of merchant and naval vessels for the Second World War. At that time the town was reckoned to be the largest shipbuilding town anywhere in the world.

As recently as 1953 there were eight Sunderland-based steel shipyards – including Pallion, which had been acquired by William Doxford & Sons Ltd in 1857 – but the 1980s brought a downturn in the industry. Wearside companies were unable to compete on the world market, particularly against companies in the Far East.

Closure of the Pallion yard saw 2,400 people lose their jobs, with many others affected in supply industries, and resulted in considerable political controversy.

(www.communigate.co.uk/ne/pallionshipyard/page1.phtml)

24 January

On this day local hero Billy Hardy narrowly failed to become Sunderland's first world boxing champion. His opponent in the International Boxing Federation Bantamweight Championship of the World at the Crowtree Leisure Centre was Orlando Canizales and after twelve rounds, it was the champion who retained his title on a split decision.

Born in Sunderland on 15 September 1964, Billy Hardy began boxing at Hylton Castle Boys' Club at the age of 6 or 7 and soon gained a reputation as an aggressive boxer who liked to take the fight to his opponent. His first professional contest, in November 1983, resulted in a 1-point victory over 6 rounds and he went on to hold the British bantamweight and featherweight championships as well as the Commonwealth featherweight title.

During his boxing career Billy Hardy fought forty-eight contests with 37 wins, 9 defeats and 2 draws and he proudly displayed his support for Sunderland Football Club by normally wearing red-and-white-striped shorts during the bouts. His achievements in the sporting world are celebrated in the name of the Billy Hardy Sports Centre in the Castleton district.

(Alan Brett, *Sunderland People and Places*, Black Cat Publications, 1990)

14 February

On this day it was officially announced that Sunderland was to be granted city status. A charter for the formation of the City of Sunderland was granted by the Crown (Head of State) to celebrate the 40th anniversary of Queen Elizabeth II's accession to the throne and it represented success in a competition in which communities were required to submit applications for city status.

The announcement was made sixty years after Sunderland submitted its first bid and followed four unsuccessful attempts. It became the 54th city in Britain at that time and with city status rarely granted, Sunderland was one of only fourteen new cities created during the twentieth century. (Contrary to popular belief, applicants do not need a cathedral within their boundaries.)

After Sunderland was granted the status of a city it gained a considerable amount of self-government and became responsible to Parliament rather than the county in which it is located. Many cities also hold the right to elect a lord mayor and most are unitary authorities.

Sunderland's successful bid was widely celebrated on Wearside and the *Sunderland Echo* funded the cost of sending commemorative letters to each of the city's 54,000 schoolchildren and full-time students.

(www.british-towns.net/england/northern/sunderland/sunderland)

10 December

On this day the last shift was completed at Wearmouth Colliery and brought to an end more than 800 years of commercial coal mining in the area. First opened in summer 1835, Wearmouth became the largest mine in the Sunderland district.

Initially the mine was under the ownership of the Pemberton family, long-established landowners in the Durham area, and the first cargo of coal was moved from the Bensham Seam (with a thickness of 5 feet 8 inches) on 18 June 1835. It had taken several years of excavation to unearth this seam at a depth of 1,590 feet below the surface and workings were gradually developed and deepened to prepare mining of the Hutton Seam at a depth of 1,722 feet.

The death of Ralph Pemberton in 1847 resulted in the sale of shares to William Bell and Partners and under their ownership it became known as the Wearmouth Colliery.

Following closure of the colliery, the site was cleared to accommodate construction of the Stadium of Light, which opened in 1997.

(www.dmm.org.uk/colliery/w001.htm)

31 July

This day saw the official opening of Sunderland AFC's Stadium of Light which featured a friendly match (scoreline 0–0) between the home team and Dutch side Ajax. Construction work had got underway during May 1996 and this fine sporting venue, with a capacity of 42,000 seats, had cost £24 million.

The choice of name – Stadium of Light – was announced only hours before the opening ceremony, which began with live performance by musicians including the rock band Status Quo and the evening's proceedings, following the first match, were brought to a close by an impressive fireworks display.

Sir Bob Murray, chairman of Sunderland AFC at that time, explained the choice of name for the stadium, which stands on the site of the Wearmouth Colliery. It was to serve as an ever-lasting tribute to the region's mineworkers and proud industrial heritage, and in expectation that the stadium would be a guiding light in the future.

The stadium's capacity was increased to 49,000 in 2002 and the original method of construction facilitated possible future expansion to 66,000. In 1999 an international friendly fixture was staged there, resulting in a 2–1 win for England over Belgium, and during 2003 England defeated Turkey 2–0 in a Euro 2004 qualifying match.

(www.stadiumguide.com/stadiumoflight/)

2 July

This day saw the closure of one of Wearside's best-known companies, Vaux Breweries, after more than 160 years of trading. Founded in 1837 by Cuthbert Vaux, it soon became a major employer in Sunderland and during 1972 the Sheffield-based Wards Brewing Company was acquired. During 1981 Vaux Breweries tried to gain a foothold in the United States with the purchase of a New York family-owned company, the Fred Koch brewery.

By the 1990s the Vaux Group had extended its business interests into hotels but the end of the decade brought a dramatic conclusion to the company's operations. During March, the Board of Directors accepted the recommendation of corporate financier B.T. Alex Brown, a subsidiary of Deutsche Bank, to close both breweries.

Company Chairman Sir Paul Nicholson had been firmly opposed to the closure and after making an unsuccessful attempt to arrange a management buyout totalling £70 million, he resigned from his post.

Six hundred jobs were lost with the closure and after the Vaux Brewery buildings were vacated they were demolished in readiness for redevelopment. Sunderland's only remaining brewery is the Bull Lane Brewing Company, based in the cellar of the Clarendon Hotel.

(news.bbc.co.uk/1/hi/business/383766.stm)

4 July

On this day a group of about fifty American descendants of the Hylton family gathered at Hylton Castle to present a flag displaying their coat of arms.

Members of the Hylton family enjoyed considerable wealth during the medieval period with estates in Yorkshire, Durham and Northumberland, and the castle was built by Sir William Hylton as his main residence in about 1400. The only section of his structure still standing is the impressive gatehouse tower, which was intended to demonstrate the family's status. Other buildings were located beyond the tower on the east side, possibly arranged around a courtyard.

The Hyltons retained their rank and wealth until the Civil War and, despite a subsequent decline in their fortunes, the family were able to make alterations to the gatehouse during the early eighteenth century. The last member of the Hylton family died in 1748 and the estate was sold off soon afterwards.

During the nineteenth century it was purchased by William Briggs, who demolished earlier extensions and redesigned the interior. Further changes of ownership saw it used briefly as a school and as a base for a local coal company.

Along with the nearby St Catherine's Chapel, Hylton Castle is now in the care of English Heritage and has Grade I status.

(www.english-heritage.org.uk/daysout/properties/
hylton-castle/history-and-research/)

3 March

On this day a blue heritage plaque was unveiled at the old Holy Trinity Rectory on Church Bank, Southwick, to highlight the building's connection with the writer Lewis Carroll. The plaque was unveiled by Sunderland's Mayor and Mayoress, Councillor Jim and Mrs Margaret Scott, and the ceremony featured a reading from one of Carroll's best-loved poems, 'The Walrus and the Carpenter'.

The event, which was part of a two-month-long local history festival organised by Sunderland Heritage Forum and the city's Library Service, represented the culmination of a campaign by Southwick History and Preservation Society to have the old rectory of Holy Trinity recognised as the place where the author visited his sister, Mary Collingwood.

It has long been known that Lewis Carroll, or Revd Charles Dodgson, spent holidays staying with his relations, Herbert and Margaret Wilcox, at their home Highcroft, in Whitburn. It is believed that he spent some time writing at cliff-top locations and even that he composed 'Jabberwocky' on the beach. While staying at Whitburn he made regular trips to see his sister, Mary, wife of the Rector of Southwick, Revd Charles Collingwood.

For many years it was believed that the Collingwoods lived at Walburn House but extensive research has verified that their home was, in fact, on Church Bank.

(Sunderland Echo)

18 April

On this day Sunderland Aquatic Centre was opened to members of the public. Completed at a cost of £20 million and located next to the Stadium of Light, it was designed by the Red Box Design Group on behalf of Sunderland City Council and represented the only facility of its kind between Leeds and Edinburgh.

Within the Aquatic Centre there was the region's only ten-lane 50-metre pool, a diving pool, gymnasium and a 25-metre multipurpose pool with springboards and diving platforms. A full range of courses and sessions were offered for all age groups and different family members, and with seating for 500 spectators it had the capacity to stage high-profile national and regional competitions.

Modern innovative features within the structure included machinery to collect, filter and then utilise rainwater in the pool, while complex insulation of the outer fabric and a combined heat and power unit maximised efficient energy usage and minimised energy waste.

Her Royal Highness the Princess Royal visited Sunderland Aquatic Centre on 22 January 2009 and a third ceremony was staged there in the presence of Mary Smith, Mayor of Sunderland, later that year. On 16 June 2012, the Olympic torch was carried through the centre as part of the Summer Olympics torch relay.

(www.bbc.co.uk/wear/content/articles/2008/01/18/aquatic_centre_feature.shtml)

24 March

A community lantern parade on this day launched three evenings of light, sound, art installations and performance at Roker Park in Sunderland. As part of the Roker by Night event, pupils from the local Redby Primary School staged promenade performances featuring the park's Spottee's Cave.

Spottee was a colourful eighteenth-century character who lived in the cave and earned a living by begging and carrying out odd jobs for local farmers. Nearby residents concluded that he was a stranded foreign seaman who could not speak English, and they gave him his unusual name because of his fondness for wearing a spotted shirt.

Mystery surrounds Spottee's eventual disappearance and it is believed that he died in the cave. In recent times the limestone cave had remained closed, but for the first night of the festival its walls were used to show archive images of Roker's history. Future plans included opening the cave as a classroom for visiting schools and for events.

Sunderland City Council had recently won £1 million from the Commission of the Architecture and the Built Environment Sea Change Fund and with an additional £500,000 from the council, work got underway to complete the first phase of improvements to Marine Walk near Roker Park.

(www.thejournal.co.uk/news/north-east-news/
lantern-parade-launched-roker-park-4437700)

14 December

Press reports on this day described a Sunderland man's amazing discovery whilst digging the garden at his home. He had arrived at the town's Museum and Winter Gardens with a football-sized bone in a carrier bag and staff soon recognised its importance. They contacted London's Natural History Museum, who confirmed that it came from an iguanodon's backbone.

Measuring around 20 centimetres in diameter, the curious bone formed part of a 10-metre-long creature which roamed the earth about 115 to 130 million years ago, but experts were mystified as to how it came to Sunderland. Rock formations in the Wearside area form part of the Permian Strata and are much too old to contain dinosaur bones. This seems to indicate that the bone was deposited there at a later date.

A spokesperson from the Natural History Museum's palae-ontology department suggested that there were two possible explanations for its appearance in Sunderland. It was either swept there by glacial transport or brought to the north east as a souvenir from England's South Coast, where iguanodon bones are often uncovered by fossil hunters.

Whatever the truth, it remains an intriguing mystery.

(*The Northern Echo*, 14 December 2011)

6 May

Sunderland's first marathon event was held on this day along a route that started and finished at the Stadium of Light. It combined with the annual Sunderland City 10k event as part of the Run Sunderland Festival and was one of a number of events held throughout the weekend.

An estimated total of 1,700 runners signed up to run the marathon, with a further 2,000 taking part in the shorter 10k run. The full course extended along the coastline at Hendon and Seaburn as well as taking in Barnes, Backhouse and Roker parks and landmarks such as Wearmouth Bridge and the National Glass Centre.

The main races took place after an afternoon of activities for young athletes that included a mini run named Niall's Mile and a *Sunderland Echo* Junior Run, held in the shadow of the Stadium of Light. Organisation of the events was in the hands of Olympic Games medallist Steve Cram, with assistance from Sally Gunnell, ambassador for the Run Sunderland Festival.

Sunderland's Marathon of the North was started by Charlie Spedding, the last Briton to win an Olympic medal in the marathon. Paul Wilson from Hartlepool won the race in a time of 2 hours 43 minutes, while the women's race was won by Susanne Hunter of Blyth Running Club with a time of 3 hours 24 minutes.

(*Sunderland Echo*)

24 May

HMS *Ocean*, the Royal Navy's largest warship, arrived in the Port of Sunderland for a special visit after the vessel and her crew had been given the Freedom of the City during 2004.

Entering the mouth of the River Wear at about 6 a.m., it was the seventh time that the warship had visited its adopted city and a programme of events was arranged for the four-day stay with the highlight taking place on Saturday, 26 May. More than 200 officers and crew marked the ship's links with Sunderland by marching through the city after a service at the city's war memorial.

Meticulous planning had ensured that the assault ship had berthed alongside the deepwater berth at Sunderland without a hitch and the vessel, which measures 208 metres (680 feet) in length, was open to the public on Sunday, 27 May. HMS *Ocean*'s commanding officer, Captain Andrew Betton, commented, 'There is a really strong and warm link between the city of Sunderland and HMS *Ocean*, which dates back to 1995 when the ship was under construction.' A member of the ship's crew said that the freedom of the city was a 'big thing' for them, as they could be respected by the people of Sunderland when they visit.

(www.bbc.co.uk/news/uk-england-tyne-18192399)

11 December

The latest stage in the revival of the Port of Sunderland was marked by the arrival of the first tugboat to take up a permanent berth in the Wear for more than twenty-five years. The *Svitzer Constance*, a 30-metre-long Voith Schneider tractor tug would play an important role in managing the increased volume of traffic arriving into Sunderland's docks. Built in 1982 by Cochrane Shipbuilders in Selby, Yorkshire, *Svitzer Constance* was considered as ideally suited to the Port of Sunderland due to its precise handling features, which enable it to manoeuvre into more confined spaces.

Middlesbrough-based Svitzer Marine Limited had made considerable investment during the vessel's earlier spell in dry dock to ensure it was suitable for operating in the port, which had seen an 84 per cent increase in traffic since 2010.

David Williams, Svitzer Marine's port manager for the north east, said:

> Over the past year we have seen Port of Sunderland really come to life and we now recognise the location as a viable base from which to operate our towing services on a permanent basis.

(www.makeitsunderland.com/index.aspx?articleid=7614)

22 June

An armada numbering more than fifty-five vessels, ranging from a 530-feet-long passenger ferry to salvage tugs and fishing trawlers, gathered along a 3-mile stretch of the North Sea to play 'Foghorn Requiem'. The hour-long score had been composed by Royal Opera House associate artist Orlando Gough and was conducted using computers that activated each vessel's foghorn. Land-based accompaniment was provided by the booming bass of Souter Lighthouse and seventy-five brass band players.

The project was assembled by artists Joshua Portway and Lise Autogena after being commissioned by the National Trust and South Tyneside Council. Opened in 1871, Souter Lighthouse was the first of its type to be powered by electricity and one of the first to have a foghorn. During the year before its construction there had been twenty wrecks along the section of coastline between the rivers Tyne and Wear.

Lighthouses in England and Wales are the responsibility of Trinity House and during recent years its officials have supervised their decommissioning. Souter was officially decommissioned in 1988 but since that time it has been maintained by volunteers from the National Trust, which operates the site.

(*Daily Telegraph*)

29 June

The National Glass Centre reopened following a £2.3 million refurbishment programme lasting six months. A new permanent exhibition entitled *Stories of Glass in Sunderland* incorporates a timeline, which shows that in 647 Benedict Biscop brought Gallic craftsmen to the monastery at Monkwearmouth to make stained-glass windows.

A glass industry subsequently developed on Wearside and after the Company of Glass Owners of Sunderland was established in 1696, there was a period of rapid growth in glassmaking. Until its closure in 1998, the local company of Hartley and Wood supplied 'antique' stained glass for buildings including Westminster Abbey, St Paul's Cathedral and the House of Commons but during 2007 the last two surviving glass firms in Sunderland, Corning Glass Works and Arc International, announced they were to close.

The centre is located on the north bank of the Wear at Monkwearmouth, where it covers the former site of J.L. Thompson & Sons shipyard. Initial building costs totalled £17 million and the official opening was performed by His Royal Highness Prince Charles during October 1998. It was the first major arts lottery award winner in the north east.

During 2010 Sunderland University took over ownership of the National Glass Centre, which accommodates its glass and ceramic course along with its arts foundation course.

(www.thejournal.co.uk/news/north-east-news/
sunderland-glass-centre-reopen-after-4712536)

28 July

The final day of Sunderland's 25th International Airshow began with a party at Cliffe Park, where live music was provided by the band of HM Royal Marines Scotland and local tribute band Re-Take That.

Damp weather marred the early stages of Europe's largest free airshow but huge crowds gathered along the coast at Seaburn and Roker to watch more than 10 hours of flying displays, which included the Battle of Britain Memorial Flight, the RAF Falcons Parachute Display Team and the Royal Navy Black Cats Solo Lynx, Tucano and Typhoon. This series of flyovers was completed by a fascinating night flight by the SWIP Twister Display Team before glittering fireworks lit up the dark skies over Wearside.

During the event there were civilian displays from SWIP Twister Display Team, the daredevil Breitling Wingwalkers, Hawker Hunter aircraft *Miss Demeanour* and the flying boat *Catalina*. A 97-year-old Second World War veteran, Lance Robson, now resident in the Morpeth area, was able to relive earlier days with a flight in the *Catalina* for the first time since 1945. The popularity of the airshow is illustrated by the fact that it was viewed online by enthusiasts in France and Oregon, USA.

(The Journal)

Bibliography

Books

Brett, Alan, *Sunderland People and Places* (Sunderland: Black Cat Publications, 1990)

Dodds, Glen Lyndon, *A History of Sunderland* (2nd edn, Sunderland: Albion Press, 2001)

Duncan, Norman, *Guide Book: St. Andrew's Church* (Sunderland: St Andrew's church, 2007)

Hudd, Roy, *Roy Hudd's Cavalcade of Variety Acts* (London: Robson Books, 1997)

Monthly Chronicle of North-Country Lore and Legend, Part LIV, August (London: W. Scott, 1981)

Richardson, M.A., *The Local Historian's Table Book, of Remarkable Occurrences, Historical Facts, Traditions, Legendary and Descriptive Ballads, &c., &c., Connected with the Counties of Newcastle-upon-Tyne, Northumberland and Durham* (Newcastle upon Tyne: M.A. Richardson, 1841–1846)

Storey, P.J., *Samuel Storey of Sunderland (1841–1925): His Life and Career as a Local Politician and Newspaper Proprietor up to 1895* (M.Litt. thesis, University of Edinburgh, 1978)

Sykes, John, *Local Records: or Historical Register of Remarkable Events Which Have Occurred Exclusively in the Counties of Durham and Northumberland, Town and County of Newcastle upon Tyne and Berwick upon Tweed; with an Obituary of Persons of Talent, Eccentricity, and Longevity* (New edn, Newcastle: T. Fordyce, 1866)

Newspapers

Daily Telegraph (London: Daily Telegraph, 1856–)

'Great Fire in Sunderland' in *Illustrated London News* (30 July 1898, p.161)

North Magazine: A Monthly Magazine For Durham, Northumberland and North Yorkshire (York, 1971–)

Sunderland Echo (Sunderland: Northeast Press, 1997–).

The Journal

The Northern Echo (Darlington: North of England Newspapers, 1870–)

The Telegraph

Websites

Bage, John, 'Pallion Shipyard: Recent History' in *This is the North East: Communigate* (2009). Available at: www.communigate.co.uk/ne/pallionshipyard/page1.phtml (Accessed 24 April 2014)

'Biography' in *Mary Stewart – A Born Storyteller* (2014). Available at: marystewartnovels.com/biography.html (Accessed 25 February 2014)

Burton, Immanuel, 'A Brief History of the Police Box', Police Boxes.com (2006). Available at: www.policeboxes.com/pboxhist.htm (Accessed 25 March 2014)

'Business: The Company File Vaux Breweries Close' in BBC News: Business (1999). Available at: news.bbc.co.uk/1/hi/business/383766.stm (Accessed 4 March 2014)

'Carnival Capers Make History' in *Sunderland Echo* (Online, 2009). Available at: www.sunderlandecho.com/news/local/all-news/carnival-capers-make-history-1-1076402 (Accessed 20 May 2014)

'The City of Sunderland', *British Towns and Villages Network* (2014). Available at: www.british-towns.net/england/northern/sunderland/sunderland (Accessed 1 April 2014)

Crosby, David, 'William Pile' in *City of Adelaide: The Splendid Clipper Ship* (2009). Available at: cityofadelaide.org.au/the-ship/the-builder.html (Accessed 18 March 2014)

'David A. Stewart' in *AllMusic* (2014). Available at: www.allmusic.com/artist/david-a-stewart-mn0000629806 (Accessed 10 March 2014)

Engineering Timelines. Available at: www.engineering-timelines.com/scripts/engineeringItem.asp?id=1134 (Accessed 11 February 2014)

Executions at Durham, 1732–1909, 'Supplied by Alistair Mills from … an unidentified newspaper' (2011). Available at: www.genuki.org.uk/big/eng/DUR/D_Executions.html (Accessed 12 February 2014)

Gould, Peter, 'Sunderland Corporation Transport, 1900–1973' (2014). Available at: www.petergould.co.uk/local_transport_history/fleetlists/sunderland1.htm (Accessed 31 March 2014)

Graham, Michael, 'Trivia Tidbits from Sunderland's Long FA Cup History' in *SB Nation Roker Report* (2012). Available at: rokerreport.sbnation.com/2012/1/24/2723573/trivia-tidbits-from-sunderlands-long-fa-cup-history (Accessed 18 March 2014)

'Hartley Wood and Co. Ltd' in The National Archives (2014). Available at: www.nationalarchives.gov.uk/a2a/records.aspx?cat=183-dshw&#0 (Accessed 24 March 2014)

Henderson, Tony, 'Lantern Parade Launched at Roker Park, Sunderland' in *The Journal* (25 March 2011) Available at: www.thejournal.co.uk/news/north-east-news/lantern-parade-launched-roker-park-4437700 (Accessed 18 March 2014)

Higginbotham, Peter, 'Sunderland, Durham' in *The Workhouse* (2014). Available at: www.workhouses.org.uk/Sunderland/ (Accessed 31 March 2014)

'History and Research: Hylton Castle' in English Heritage. Available at:
www.english-heritage.org.uk/daysout/properties/hylton-castle/
history-and-research/ (Accessed 18 March 2014)

'HMS *Ocean* Arrives in Sunderland for Special Visit' in BBC News: Tyne
& Wear (2012). Available at: www.bbc.co.uk/news/uk-england-
tyne-18192399 (Accessed: 25 February 2014)

Hutchinson, Lisa, 'Sunderland Airshow is off to a Flying Start' in
The Journal (12 July 2013). Available at: www.thejournal.co.uk/news/
north-east-news/sunderland-airshow-flying-start-5071537
(Accessed 11 May 2014)

'Jack Crawford: The Hero From Pottery Bank' in Sunderland Antiquarian
Society (2008). Available at: www.sunderland-antiquarians.org/
members-area/jack-crawford (Accessed 24 March 2014)

'John Grimshaw, Rope-making. Genius at Sunderland near Newcastle
Upon Tyne', Grimshaw Origins and History (2012). Available
at: www.grimshaworigin.org/JohnGwRopemaker.htm
(Accessed: 24 March 2014)

'Kate Adie' in BBC News: On This Day: Correspondents (2014).
Available at: news.bbc.co.uk/onthisday/hi/correspondents/
newsid_2625000/2625875.stm (Accessed 10 March 2014)

Kilpatrick, Alison, 'News extracts: Oct. 7, 1824: D. M'Donald invented
a "self-moving carriage", at Sunderland' in RootsWeb GENBRIT-L
Archives (7 October 2008). Available at: archiver.rootsweb.ancestry.com/
th/read/GENBRIT/2008-10/1223366508 (Accessed 19 June 2014)

'The Lords of the North' in Living North (2014). Available at:
www.livingnorth.com/northeast/sport/lords-north (Accessed 7 May 2014)

Lloyd, Matthew, 'Sunderland Theatres and Halls' in arthurlloyd.co.uk
The Music Hall and Theatre History Website (2014). Available at:
www.arthurlloyd.co.uk/Sunderland.htm (Accessed 12 February 2014)

'Mary Ann Cotton' in Murderpedia (2014). Available at:
murderpedia.org/female.C/c/cotton-mary-ann.htm (Accessed 4 June 2014)

Mason, Barbara, 'Sunderland has Become a Literary Wonderland' in
NorthEastLife (2012). Available at: www.northeastlifemag.co.uk/out-about/
places/sunderland_has_become_a_literary_wonderland_1_1569407
(Accessed 25 March 2014)

McKinstry, Leo, 'Sid James the Crimper who Became Carry On's King' in
Daily Express (Saturday 4 May 2013). Available at:
www.express.co.uk/news/uk/396943/Sid-James-the-crimper-who-
became-Carry-On-s-king (Accessed 12 February 2014)

Monkwearmouth Station Museum, 'Local Studies Centre Fact Sheet 17'
(Sunderland, Sunderland City Council). Available at:
www.sunderland.gov.uk/CHttpHandler.ashx?id=6951
(Accessed 18 March 2014)

Moore, Randy, 'William Paley, 1743–1805' in *Reports of the National Centre for
Science Education*, Vol. 29, (July–August 2009, pp. 26–7). Available at: ncse.
com/rncse/29/4/william-paley-1743-1805 (Accessed 6 May 2014)

Mowbray Park, 'Local Studies Centre Fact Sheet 2', Sunderland,
    Sunderland City Council. Available at: www.sunderland.gov.uk/
    CHttpHandler.ashx?id=6912 (Accessed 18 May 2014)
'Nat Jackley' in Answers.com (2014). Available at:
    www.answers.com/topic/nat-jackley-1 (Accessed 5 June 2014)
Northern Archaeological Associates, 'Project Profile: Roker Pier
    and Lighthouse' in *NAA Heritage Consultants* (2013). Available
    at: northernarchaeologicalassociates.co.uk/profile/44-RP.htm
    (Accessed 10 March 2014)
Ord, Richard, 'The Clipper Ship *Torrens'* in *Sunderland Echo* (16 April 2008)
    Available at: www.sunderlandecho.com/opinion/columnists/the-clipper-
    ship-torrens-1-1147795 (Accessed 25 March 2014)
'Park Road Methodist Church (1887)' in Sunderland Heritage Forum (2014).
    Available at: www.sunderlandheritage.org.uk/buildings.php?id=82
    (Accessed 6 May 2014)
'People & Parliament Transforming Society' in Living Heritage
    (2014). Available at: www.parliament.uk/about/living-heritage/
    transformingsociety/towncountry/ (Accessed 24 February 2014)
Plant, David, 'Civil War in the North, 1644' in BCW Project, (2006).
    Available at: bcw-project.org/military/english-civil-war/northern-
    england/the-north-1644 (Accessed 13 May 2014)
'Queen Alexandra Bridge' in *Sunderland History* (2014). Available at:
    www.sunderlandhistory.co.uk/River-Wear-ID6/Bridges-IDS7/Queen-
    Alexandra-Bridge-IDI23 (Accessed 7 May 2014)
'R.A.M.C. profile of George Allan Maling' in *RAMC in the Great War*
    (2014). Available at: www.ramc-ww1.com/profile.php?profile_id=11778
    (Accessed 25 February 2014)
Routledge, Martin, 'Monkwearmouth Station Bombed!' in Tyne & Wear
    Archives & Museums (2012). Available at: www.twmuseums.org.uk/engage/
    blog/monkwearmouth-station-bombed/ (Accessed 18 March 2014)
Routledge, Martin, 'The Newbottle Waggon Rail Way Map' in Tyne & Wear
    Archives & Museums (2013). Available at: www.twmuseums.org.uk/engage/
    blog/the-newbottle-waggon-rail-way-map/ (Accessed 24 February 2014)
Ryhope Engines Museum (2014). Available at: www.ryhopeengines.org.uk/
    (Accessed 13 May 2014)
'Shipwrecks' The Sunderland site. Available at: www.searlecanada.org/
    sunderland/sunderland015.html (Accessed 5 June 2014)
'Shocks do happen' in The FA cup and Competitions (2014). Available at:
    www.thefa.com/competitions/facompetitions/thefacup/history/
    historyofthefacup/1973sunderlandleeds (Accessed 11 March 2014)
Simkin, John, 'Charles William Alcock' in Football Encyclopaedia
    (2013). Available at: www.spartacus.schoolnet.co.uk/FalcockC.htm
    (Accessed 24 February 2014)
'Sir Joseph Wilson Swan' in Encyclopaedia Britannica (2013). Available at:
    www.britannica.com/EBchecked/topic/576273/Sir-Joseph-Wilson-
    Swan (Accessed 3 March 2014)

'Sir Tom Cowie' in *The Telegraph* Obituaries (2012). Available at: www.telegraph.co.uk/news/obituaries/9045286/Sir-Tom-Cowie.html (Accessed 3 March 2014)

'St. Benedict Biscop' in Encyclopaedia Britannica (2001). Available at: www.britannia.com/bios/saints/benedictbiscop.html (Accessed 23 April 2014)

'Stadium of Light' in The Stadium Guide (2014). Available at: www.stadiumguide.com/stadiumoflight/ (Accessed 26 February 2014)

Stoner, Sarah, 'Wearside Echoes: How Sunderland Celebrated Queen Victoria's Diamond Jubilee' in *Sunderland Echo* (27 May 2012). Available at: www.sunderlandecho.com/history-nostalgia/wearside-echoes-how-sunderland-celebrated-queen-victoria-s-diamond-jubilee-1-4590465 (Accessed 18 March 2014)

'Sunderland Aquatic Centre' in BBC: Wear (2008). Available at: www.bbc.co.uk/wear/content/articles/2008/01/18/aquatic_centre_feature.shtml (Accessed: 5 June 2014)

'Sunderland A.F.C.' in Wikipedia (2014). Available at: en.wikipedia.org/wiki/Sunderland_A.F.C. (Accessed 1 April 2014)

'Sunderland Echo' in Wikipedia (2014). Available at: en.wikipedia.org/wiki/Sunderland_Echo (Accessed 21 April 2014)

Sunderland Orphan Asylum (1861)' Sunderland Heritage Forum (2014). Available at: www.sunderlandheritage.org.uk/buildings.php?id=95 (Accessed 6 May 2014)

Sunderland's Music, Arts and Culture Quarter (2014). Available at: www.macq.org.uk/the-history/ (Accessed 4 June 2014)

'Sunderland's shipyards during WW2' in BBC: Legacies Wear (2004). Available at: www.bbc.co.uk/legacies/work/england/wear/article_1.shtml (Accessed 25 March 2014)

'Sunderland Station' in Wikipedia (2014). Available at: en.wikipedia.org/wiki/Sunderland_station (Accessed 13 May 2014)

'Sunderland Volunteer Life Brigade – Rescues' in Sunderland Volunteer Life Brigade (2014). Available at: www.sunderlandvlb.com/rescues.php (Accessed 4 June 2014)

'Svitzer Constance Sails into Port of Sunderland' in MAKE it Sunderland (2012). Available at: www.makeitsunderland.com/index.aspx?articleid=7614 (Accessed 20 May 2014)

'Tyne and Wear HER (13559): Sunderland, Holmeside, No. 42, Black's Regal Cinema – Details', Sitelines (2014). Available at: www.twsitelines.info/smr/13559 (Accessed 5 June 2014)

'Tyne and Wear Sunderland, Sunderland Civic Centre', Royal Commission on the Ancient and Historical Monuments of Scotland, Canmore (2014). Available at: canmore.rcahms.gov.uk/en/site/284670/details/tyne+and+wear+sunderland+sunderland+civic+centre/ (Accessed 20 May 2014)

University of Sunderland: Our History, University of Sunderland (2013). Available at: www.sunderland.ac.uk/university/factsandfigures/ourhistory/ (Accessed 1 April 2014)

'Was the Cauld Lad Murdered After All?' in *Sunderland Echo* (2007). Available at: www.sunderlandecho.com/what-s-on/was-the-cauld-lad-murdered-after-all-1-1141690 (Accessed 3 June 2014)

'Wearmouth Colliery' in Durham Mining Museum (2014). Available at: www.dmm.org.uk/colliery/w001.htm (Accessed 24 April 2014)

'Wearside Echoes: Fun at the Y.M.C.A.' in *Sunderland Echo* (2011). Available at: www.sunderlandecho.com/history-nostalgia/wearside-echoes-fun-at-the-ymca-1-4052077 (Accessed 3 June 2014)

Whetstone, David, 'Sunderland Glass Centre to reopen after £2.3m redevelopment' in *The Journal* (26 June 2013). Available at: www.thejournal.co.uk/news/north-east-news/sunderland-glass-centre-reopen-after-4712536 (Accessed 11 March 2014)

Whitehead, Tony, 'Colliery Railways: Hetton Colliery Railway', Durham Records Online (2013). Available at: durhamrecordsonline.com/library/hetton-colliery-railway/ (Accessed 25 March 2014)

'William Mills (inventor)' in Wikipedia (2014). Available at: en.wikipedia.org/wiki/William_Mills_(inventor) (Accessed 6 May 2014)

About the Author

Robert Woodhouse taught in schools for over thirty-five years before retiring, and currently tutors adults in local history courses throughout the north east. He is the author of thirty-five books on regional history.